W9-CHZ-096

Radical Inclusion

Radical
Inclusion

Seven Steps
to Help You Create
a More Just Workplace,
Home, and World

David Moinina Sengeh

MOMENT
OF LIFT
BOOKS

FLATIRON
BOOKS
NEW YORK

This is a work of nonfiction. Dialogue has been reconstructed to the best of the author's ability. Some names have been changed, along with potentially identifying characteristics.

RADICAL INCLUSION. Copyright © 2023 by David Moinina Sengeh. All rights reserved. Printed in the United States of America. For information, address Flatiron Books, 120 Broadway, New York, NY 10271.

An extension of this copyright page appears on page 239.

www.flatironbooks.com

Designed by Donna Sinisgalli Noetzel

Library of Congress Cataloging-in-Publication Data

Names: Sengeh, David Moinina, author.
Title: Radical inclusion : seven steps toward creating a more just society / David Moinina Sengeh.
Description: First edition. | New York : Flatiron Books, 2023. | Includes bibliographical references.
Identifiers: LCCN 2022054325 | ISBN 9781250827746 (hardcover) | ISBN 9781250827753 (ebook)
Subjects: LCSH: Girls—Education—Sierra Leone. | Pregnant teenagers—Education—Sierra Leone. | Right to education—Sierra Leone. | Educational change—Sierra Leone. | Social justice and education—Sierra Leone.
Classification: LCC LC2477.95 .S46 2023 | DDC 371.82209664—dc23/eng/20221214
LC record available at https://lccn.loc.gov/2022054325

Our books may be purchased in bulk for promotional, educational, or business use. Please contact your local bookseller or the Macmillan Corporate and Premium Sales Department at 1-800-221-7945, extension 5442, or by email at MacmillanSpecialMarkets@macmillan.com.

First Edition: 2023

10 9 8 7 6 5 4 3 2 1

To the memories of
Dr. J. C. Boima and P. J. Mandewa-Cole,
who both showed me how to live a life
of service to Sierra Leone;

and to my daughters,
Peynina Athena Krontiris-Sengeh, Nyaanina Sophia
Krontiris-Sengeh, and Kadija Davida Conteh,
and all schoolgirls who inspire me
to live a life of service to humanity

Contents

· · · · ·

Author's Note

You Are Not Included

· · · · ·

You are not included. No matter what your economic status, your social capital, your race, or your position may be, you are likely to face exclusion at some time in your life.

In February 2022, Queen Elizabeth II celebrated her Platinum Jubilee, the seventieth anniversary of her ascent to the throne. But just a few months later, in May, she was not able to deliver her annual speech at the State Opening of Parliament for the first time in more than fifty years. When her crown was ceremonially placed on a stool and Prince Charles read her speech, the reason for her absence was revealed: "episodic mobility issues." In simpler terms, her disabilities. The queen sadly passed away in September 2022.

We as a world have not yet found a way to welcome and accept people with disabilities in every room—even someone who was arguably the most powerful and beloved person in the United Kingdom. There were suggestions that the royal family and the queen herself were embarrassed that she would have had to use a wheelchair in public, which underscores the magnitude of the challenges around disability rights and justice.

So many people with disabilities are not seen. If you live with any form of disability, you are not included, even if you are the queen of England.

Many years ago, my mentor and friend Professor Henry Louis Gates, Jr., returned from a trip to China to find that the door to his home in Cambridge, Massachusetts, was jammed shut. When he and his driver tried to force it open, a neighbor called the police to report a burglary. Though Gates was clearly the homeowner, he was arrested and taken into custody for disorderly conduct. Class, income, and fame are not deterrents to racial bias. In the eyes of the police, Gates was not a Harvard professor; he was just a Black man and hence a likely criminal. Many professional people of color experience their lowest moments at the zeniths of their careers, when systemic racism kicks in to remind them of how little regard so many people have for their accomplishments. It is often argued that overt racism in America and around the world actually *increased* after Barack Obama, a Black man, was elected president. If you are a person of color or a member of a minority group, you are often not included, and depending on where you live, your safety is not guaranteed.

In Tanzania, Gambia, Uganda, and several other countries, including Sierra Leone until March 2020, girls are not allowed or supported to attend school if they are visibly pregnant. And that is just the tip of the iceberg of the inequities girls experience because of their gender. By the time they are adults, they will be at greater risk of sexual violence, receive less pay, and enjoy less social status than their male counterparts. If you are a woman, you are not included.

As serious a problem as systemic exclusion is, it is our inability to recognize it that perpetuates the continued lack of justice in the world. Once we recognize this exclusion, we might see that we ourselves belong to the group that enforces it, either directly or through our inaction. That's the first step, but what comes next? How do we go about fighting for inclusion and justice? What tools can we use to identify and name the exclusion, listen and learn about the issues, understand whatever role we play in them, form a coalition, take action, and consolidate whatever progress we've made before repeating the process again and again?

This book offers some guidelines, by showing how we worked to change the policy that excluded thousands of pregnant girls from attending school in Sierra Leone. It's my hope that by reading a story about the efforts we made to right a very specific wrong, you can gain some insight and maybe even inspiration that will help you in your own efforts to create a more just society in your home, your community, your school, your workplace, and your country.

It is only when we truly believe in and practice radical inclusion—a commitment to keep fighting for everyone to be included, no matter who they are, where they come from, and how they show up—that we can begin to experience justice in the world.

Introduction

The Need for Radical Inclusion

. . . . .

*Feet, what do I need you for when I have
wings to fly?*

—FRIDA KAHLO

In the summer of 2004, when I was still a teenager, I went to
the Freetown International Airport in Lungi, Sierra Leone, to
board my first international flight to Abidjan in Côte d'Ivoire.
I had received a scholarship to attend the Red Cross Nordic
United World College in Norway that fall. Since there was
no way to obtain a visa in Sierra Leone, citizens—those who
could afford to—went either to Ghana, Guinea, Senegal, or
Côte d'Ivoire to get one. It was my second time on an airplane,
but the experience this time was completely different. That

first flight had been from Freetown, where I was attending secondary school, to my hometown of Bo to visit my mother. It was in the late 1990s, during the peak of Sierra Leone's eleven-year civil war. The 151-mile route between the two cities was filled with roadblocks manned by armed rebels; driving cross-country could easily be a death sentence.

That first time I flew, I knew my mother would be waiting to greet me with a hug at the dusty airfield in Bo; this time, there would be no one waiting for me on the tarmac. After I arrived in Abidjan, I remember being scared and uncertain, but also curious. I felt like an outsider (which I was), but I opened myself up to the generosity of strangers, and I was helped at every turn.

The Red Cross Nordic United World College is one of eighteen schools on four continents that bring students together from all over the world. Everything about living in Norway—the food, the music, the language, the culture—was foreign to me. For starters, I found myself shivering violently in the cold as soon as I stepped off the plane, even though I was wearing a suit—and it was still summer. Each of my new schoolmates, 199 young people from ninety different countries, had their own story of how they had come to be in Flekke, a small village amid the fjords of southwestern Norway. Mine was rather straightforward: I had gone through public secondary school, done well in my national exams, and been awarded an academic scholarship. While each of the participating schools focused on diversity and promoted peace and sustainability through education, I had chosen to go to Norway precisely because it was so different from Sierra Leone. I thought different was cool.

During my travels to and from Norway and throughout Europe over the next two years, I was often the only Sierra Leonean in the queues at the border control kiosks. Almost every time, I was pulled aside for extra questioning. It was as if I'd misread the green sign on the lane that said EXIT. NOTH-ING TO DECLARE. The first and second times I was pulled into a small room and asked to open my bag for inspection I assumed it was routine, but by the sixth, seventh, and eighth times, I knew there was nothing random about my selection. When I compared notes with other students, I discovered that most of my Black and African friends had had similar experiences. That was when I first began to understand that different wasn't always pleasant. One time, frustrated by this perceived injustice, I chose the STOP. SOMETHING TO DECLARE lane, even though I had nothing to declare. Since they were going to pull me aside anyway, I thought, why not make it easier for them, and save myself the time and the worry? Several hours of questioning later, I decided not to use that strategy again in the future.

Sometimes the officers who questioned me were cradling

their rifles in their arms. I'll never be comfortable around guns because of what I experienced during the civil war, but I tried to stay as calm as I could—to not make any wrong moves or say the wrong things—because I knew that any misunderstanding could have deadly consequences. This was something my mom explicitly warned me about when we fled Bo when it was attacked in the late nineties. She knew my penchant for asking questions and challenging authority. "The person with the gun in hand is always right," she'd said. Instead, I tried to turn those stressful interrogations into learning opportunities.

It was a skill that would come in handy a couple of years later when I came to the United States. When I matriculated at Harvard College in 2006, I was the only student directly from Sierra Leone. After I received my undergraduate degree, I pursued graduate studies at the Massachusetts Institute of Technology (MIT) before moving to Nairobi, Kenya, for work. Throughout my academic and professional career, living and working in Norway, the United States, Kenya, and South Africa, I have been either actively or indirectly forced to recognize that I am different countless times.

Looking back today, I can see that I shouldn't have been surprised. I was a young, Black Sierra Leonean man with blond-tinted dreadlocks, studying biomechatronics at institutions far away from my home. Most of the people I spent my time with did not look or talk like me. Still, I tried very hard to be included. That made it all the more painful when I did not succeed, but it also gave me empathy for other Sierra Leonean young men, who looked and talked like me, but had been left on the margin because they'd lost limbs during our brutal civil war.

I decided to use technology to help them and other people with physical disabilities be more included. For my doctoral work at MIT, I combined multi-material 3-D printing, magnetic resonance imaging, and soft tissue modeling to create novel prostheses. The work attracted notice and in 2014 I was invited to co-host TEDMED—one of the world's biggest medical conferences—at the John F. Kennedy Center for the Performing Arts in Washington, D.C. But what I'd hoped would be a joyful event provided yet another lesson in exclusion.

After my talk on the main stage, I was accosted by a drunk on the street just a few blocks from the Kennedy Center. To my surprise, he correctly identified my accent. "Go back to West Africa!" he shouted. "Go back to Sierra Leone where you came from!" I felt angry, humiliated, and also scared for my safety, as he was brandishing a bottle. I thought about the news headline that my mother would read (if it even made the news) should the situation escalate any further: UNARMED BLACK MAN KILLED IN WASHINGTON, D.C. One of the friends I was walking with—a tall white man with a well-built frame from playing lacrosse—stepped in, told him to cut it out, and scared him away. But at the exact moment that I should have felt not just included but embraced by American society, I had been made to feel the opposite.

Of course, I knew that I was far from alone.

If you watched the news any time over the last few years, even for just a few minutes, you would have seen any number of stories about the world's seemingly irreversible social inequities. In America, Black people were protesting the racial injustices they experienced day in and day out. In Great Britain, there were bitter debates for and against Brexit, most of which turned on who belonged and who needed to be kept out. The cry for inclusion and equity led to major political shifts, some of them positive, and many for the worse. Far-right groups that promote hate, division, and violence became increasingly visible and influential, even in once-stable European democracies.

Inclusion has become a subject of extensive scholarly research. It's hard to find any modern global institution that doesn't list it as one of their organizational values. Debates about exclusion and inclusion can tear families apart—or bring whole societies together.

Almost by definition, someone in every group feels excluded sometimes, for any number of reasons. The inclusion-exclusion

6

border is fluid. No one is on one side of it at all times; but across domains, some people are more often excluded than others.

The one thing that's guaranteed is that everyone involved in exclusion—whether included or excluded—is affected by it, even if they don't know it. A positive way to look at it is that when we build inclusive solutions, we all benefit, even if we do not know it. As a simple example, wheelchair ramps that increase accessibility for people living with disabilities are also used by parents of all socioeconomic classes pushing baby strollers.

In these debates about inclusion, some people are vocal, some are silent, and many more are in between. There are activists on both sides whose positions, as often as not, are as deeply rooted in history, culture, religion, and tradition as they are in the realities of modern-day life and politics. Whether through legacy systems, legislation, bureaucracy, or just plain hatred for our human differences, systemic exclusion persists and is deepened and made more intractable by the widening socioeconomic disparities that exist in all societies. Social media provides a platform for the most extreme views. If not addressed, systemic exclusion will continue to divide us, leaving us ever more vulnerable to global crises like climate change, pandemics, and threats to our physical and digital security.

This book addresses inclusion, but it is not about its history or science. Its aim is to offer us, as individuals and as a society, some insights into why the fight against exclusion is so important, and a set of tools that can help us if we choose to join it.

I am not suggesting that everyone should believe in the same things. In fact, quite the opposite: research from the world of business and management shows that teams perform much better when they are diverse, and not just in gender, race, language, and all the other crucial aspects of identity that so often divide us, but in opinions and life philosophies. Inclusion as a social construct is about accepting everyone and recognizing all they can contribute to our homes, schools, and communities—not irrespective of their differences, but *because* of them. On the flip side, exclusion levies emotional, financial, social, and other costs that affect not just those who are excluded, but those who exclude and work to keep that exclusion in place. The more inclusive a society, the more it is perceived as a just society; and just societies are safer for everyone. Simply put, the pursuit of inclusion is in everyone's interest.

But achieving inclusion is not easy. The topic often feels impossible to address; it is easier to ignore the exclusion and its associated inequities than to fix it. That's why so many of us hesitate to intervene when a child with a physical disability is left out of a playground game. Or why too few of us speak up to counter sexist statements in boardrooms, even when it's clear that many of those present are uncomfortable. Or why we join in the laughter, however awkwardly, when a friend in a bar makes a bad joke about gay people or a woman's place being in the kitchen.

It's why so many of us engage in "code-switching." Code-switching is when individuals change who they are—how they talk, dress, or show up—so they can feel *seen* and feel a sense of belonging. This solution is often necessary for survival, but it can carry a high emotional cost. I know that because I've practiced it throughout my life. It's a temporary solution to a permanent problem. To achieve lasting change, new policies have to be instituted and societies have to shift so that we can be who we are wherever we are, unless we freely choose otherwise.

What we need is radical inclusion, and that cannot be achieved with inaction and silence. We need to take committed actions that drive us toward it. To get at this, I want to share a very specific story with you, about a time in my life when I was called to action and felt I had to speak and act up.

I had left Sierra Leone alone but returned with a wife and a young daughter. In 2018, when I was thirty-one, I was appointed by His Excellency Brigadier General (Retired) Dr. Julius Maada Bio, the president of the Republic of Sierra Leone, as the government of Sierra Leone's first chief innovation officer.

A year later, in 2019, I became Sierra Leone's youngest-ever minister of basic and senior secondary education.

The two institutions I lead directly serve more than three million people. Both enjoy great autonomy and receive substantial budgetary allocations. I saw my cabinet position in education and my role as the nation's chief innovation officer as exciting opportunities for me to transform the future for my children and all the other children in Sierra Leone through the power of technology and education. But on the very same day that I took my oath of office as cabinet minister, President Bio unknowingly and unintentionally threw me the most important professional and personal challenge I'd ever faced. He announced to the world that his government, of which I now was a part, would uphold a policy that banned visibly pregnant girls from attending school, which had been passed into law ten years before.

What in the world? I thought to myself. How could I enforce such an unjust law when I had two beautiful daughters of my own? (My second child was born in June 2019.) As someone who had felt excluded himself, and whose academic research was devoted to inclusive technology, it was out of the question. For a moment, I thought about walking away from what until that minute had been my dream job. But if I did, then who would fight for those pregnant girls who simply wanted to learn? I had known the ban existed before I took the job, of course, but I had never dreamed that the president I so admired would want to continue it.

In the chapters that follow, I will tell you how I worked with the president, his government, the ministry, and my fellow citizens in the fight to overturn the ban. The path was neither clear nor linear; I wasn't sure if, how, or when our efforts would succeed. But what I came to discover, through very painful trials and many errors, was the approach that I have distilled into what I now call the Seven Principles of Radical Inclusion.

People around the globe are working to build more inclusive environments, addressing racial biases, religious intolerance, gender discrimination, migration, security, and climate change, among countless other inequities and issues. In order to succeed, these movements must transcend individuals. However, they are often pioneered and powered by individuals or small groups of people who dedicate their lives, resources, and time toward inclusion. Some of them will stop at nothing, often fighting to their graves until the change they pursue happens. I've tried throughout these pages to pay tribute to these heroes. But I also have attempted to highlight the contributions of others who mobilize every day to take seemingly small actions in their homes, schools, and communities—like building a sidewalk ramp for a neighbor who uses a wheelchair, setting up rules that allow all voices to be heard at public meetings, or helping a visually impaired classmate navigate the uneven paths that cross a campus. I've learned and am still learning from all of them; my hope is that the principles of radical inclusion will serve as a guide for anyone who joins the fight.

Radical inclusion is radical because it involves a commitment to intentional and persistent action and seeks to help all people who have been excluded, directly or indirectly, due to the tides of history, current actions or inactions, unjust laws, systemic inequities, or reasons that are hard to pinpoint but nonetheless exist.

Radical inclusion isn't a destination. It's a journey where the best you can do is to try to get ever closer to the destination, which is a more just society. The principles are also steps, and while they don't need to happen in the sequence I've presented, aspects of each are necessary for inspiring and driving lasting change.

The Seven Principles of Radical Inclusion

1. **Identify the exclusion:** You cannot promote an agenda of inclusion if you do not identify, name, and recognize all the ways in which people are excluded, as well as the associated impacts and costs of that exclusion. You must

define your terms precisely if you are to see the opportunities that exist for solving the problem.

2. **Listen, to understand and learn:** You have to listen to understand how everyone, including the perpetrators, the advocates, the victims, and the silent observers feel; how they are impacted by and how they benefit from exclusion in society. Only then can you begin to build a case for radical inclusion that works for everyone. Oftentimes, the ones you disagree with the most are the ones you should listen to the most attentively.

3. **Define your role—why you, why now?** You must define the role of all actors—active and silent—both those who are fighting to maintain the status quo, and those who are working to change it. And you must look unblinkingly at yourself. What is it about you and the situation at this time and this location that make it possible for change to occur?

4. **Build a coalition:** You cannot change systems that are rooted in history and culture by yourself. For radical shifts to occur, you need to identify and mobilize a critical mass of allies. You need as many people and institutions to work and fight beside you as you can find.

5. **Advocacy and action:** Taking action is the most direct way to enable inclusion. In fact, it is the only way;

silent advocacy is not an option. You must make a commitment to take the sustained actions that are needed to remove the exclusion you have identified.

6. **Adapting to a new normal:** Because change is new, it can be difficult. To make the inclusion permanent, everyone—both the previous excluder and the newly included—needs a framework to respond to, accept, and be a part of the "new normal."

7. **Beyond inclusion:** Once the previously identified exclusion has been eliminated and the new normal established, the best way to solidify it is to immediately identify the next exclusion that needs to be addressed, whether in your home, school, community, nation, or the world at large. We must always be working toward a more just society by identifying new areas of exclusion and dismantling them through radical inclusion.

The fight for inclusion is not easy but it is deeply fulfilling. To borrow words of wisdom from a leader who not only devoted his life to the fight for inclusion but died in it, Martin Luther King, Jr., once said, "The arc of the moral universe is long, but it bends toward justice." In our efforts to reverse the ban against pregnant girls attending school and to build a more inclusive education agenda in Sierra Leone, we went against the largest and most dominant social constructs in our society. The stories I will tell are filled with examples of courage and perseverance, examples that I hope will inspire you. (I have changed the names of some of the people in them, as a courtesy.) When coordinated action is directed toward a shared goal, justice will prevail in time. Someday, perhaps, we will live in a world where no one is made to feel left out, and most important, where no one feels the need to make others feel left out.

1

Identify the Exclusion

. . . . .

*You can't understand most of the important things
from a distance. . . . You have to get close.*

—BRYAN STEVENSON

At home in Sierra Leone, I hardly ever use an alarm clock.
When I'm visiting rural communities, I'm more likely to be
woken up by the *kokorioko* sound of a chicken, the melodious
calls of songbirds, or the Muslim *azaan,* the call to prayer. In
my neighborhood in Freetown what usually rouses me is the
deep baritone of a bread seller singing "*tapalapa* two thousand," a man preaching the Gospel of the Lord through a
megaphone as he walks down the middle of the street, or the

beeping horn and revving motor of an *okada* (motorcycle taxi) transporting early risers to work.

Once roused, I open one eye and reach for my phone, which is usually lying on top of whatever book happens to be sitting on the white table on my side of the bed. Squinting against the light shining through the thin white linen curtains, I turn it on and start browsing through the headlines. Most mornings I am interrupted by a knock on the door before I can click on any of the stories, and a chorus of tiny voices shouting *"Dadaaaa, bu waa!"* ("Good morning, Daddy!"). As soon as I hear that, I slide my phone under the pillow and lift the blue mosquito net that hangs over the bed so our two children—Nyaanina Sophia, now seven years old, and her sister Peynina Athena, three and a half years younger—can join us. Both love their morning routine, which includes tight hugs and cuddles mixed with tickle attacks and laughter. Nyaanina and Peynina are similar in many ways, yet also very different, so their routines vary accordingly. Nyaanina describes herself as a "love person"; she could easily spend hours expressing and receiving affection, so she gets a longer cuddle. Peynina is eager to begin her daily explorations of the house, so she only wants a quick hug and a kiss on her forehead. Their older teenage cousin, fourteen-year-old Kadija, often follows them into the room and whisks them away to breakfast. Kadija is my elder sister's oldest daughter but I treat her as if she were one of my own. She moved in with us soon after we returned to Sierra Leone because space in her parents' home was tight. Also, we wanted our girls to grow up amongst extended family and my sister wanted the same for Kadija.

Breakfast, like every meal chez Krontiris-Sengeh, is an event. My wife, Kate Krontiris, is a social scientist and trained facilitator. That means discussion and debate are always on the menu, no matter the time of day, and everyone is expected to participate fully, even Peynina. Kate and I first met at MIT where we were graduate students. Kate was part of the MIT Africa team that had invited me to speak in the spring of 2012 on the topic of African Youth: Entrepreneurship and Education. Kate and I started dating right after that conference and got married three years later. Those topics have remained constant themes for debate in our home as my life's work has revolved around them.

My workday is typically between nine and ten hours and, unlike my mornings with my girls at home, it is anything but routine. As cabinet minister, I engage with a cross section of stakeholders including representatives from teacher organizations, civil society institutions, and development partners, and parents who, I'm glad to say, often take me up on my open-door policy. The meetings only stop when I leave my office to attend an external event or make a surprise visit to a school. During those school visits, I regularly find myself at the blackboard teaching. I try to connect with students as often as I can, to better understand their daily realities. In the midst of all this, I'm always on standby to attend a meeting with the president or one of his delegates since, as chief innovation officer, I am his primary adviser on science, technology, and innovation.

I'm quite mindful of the clock during the day because it's very important to me to be home on time for dinner. Kate, Kadija, Nyaanina, and Peynina usually wait for me to get home so we can eat as a family. We use that time to debrief one another about our days and also debate about topics that concern us. Nyaanina loves being the one to ask, "What's your peach and what's your pit?"

In between the start and end of my days, my mind is fully dedicated to work. I try to be fully present at home, although I'm not always successful at that since my work does follow me everywhere. Kate usually makes a point of reminding me to log off and leave my phone far away from the dining table and our bed, but as evidenced by my morning scroll through the headlines, it's a challenge I'm still working on. I'm successful sometimes, but when I'm not it causes understandable tension and unhappiness.

On the evening of November 20, 2019, when Kate asked me, "How was your day?" I had plenty to tell her. And it wasn't good.

That morning, less than twenty-four hours after I had been approved by the Parliament of Sierra Leone to be the new cabinet minister in charge of the Ministry of Basic and Senior Secondary Education, and just hours after I'd been sworn in, I'd slipped into the back of the Freetown International Conference Centre to attend an event. I was a bit late because I'd been meeting my new staff, and the speeches were already underway. On the agenda was a commemoration of World Children's Day, and then our new president, Julius Maada Bio, would deliver the keynote address.

Students, teachers, civil society organization representatives, diplomats, and heads of development partner organizations all sat quietly in the dimly lit, jam-packed room to listen to the president's speech on the status of children and their right to education in Sierra Leone. I was physically in the room, but I wasn't fully present.

My mind was stuck on the image of a girl we had driven past on the way to the convention center. Although my SUV's dark-tinted windows were closed, I could tell it was windy outside because her long purple skirt was billowing. Her hair was finely plaited and her face shiny and well oiled. Had her skirt not had a flowery pattern, I would have assumed she was wearing a uniform and on her way to school. She waved for us to slow down, and my driver stopped to let her cross the road. As she paused in front of our vehicle to let an *okada* in

21

the opposite traffic lane pass, I noticed she was pregnant. She couldn't have been any older than sixteen—about the same age as the schoolgirl I happened to be sitting next to in the auditorium. She could have been attending the same school as my niece Kadija, I thought. How did she get pregnant, and how was her family and society advocating for her future? Under the current government policy, she wasn't allowed to attend school and I wondered if she would ever go back. Thank goodness, I thought, that the policy would soon be overturned.

Girls and young women face unique challenges, whether in Sierra Leone, Nigeria, the United Kingdom, or elsewhere, that prevent them from safely accessing classes, staying in school, and obtaining quality education. In many places, girls, or certain groups of girls, are denied access to education purely because of their gender, depriving them of their best opportunity for improving their lives, and perpetuating the cycle of intergenerational poverty. The problem had been at the back of my mind for years. Until the challenge it poses to equity and justice is addressed, development at local, national, and global levels will be stunted. Finally, I was in a position to do something—something radical—about girls' educations.

When a group of people are excluded or feel excluded, they often don't even have the language to express the challenges they experience, never mind the power to change their situation. Exclusion is almost always about power and the need to retain it. Sometimes the actions that lead to others being excluded are not intentional; they may seem mundane or normal, like one kid making fun of another's speech impairment, mimicking the way the other child mispronounces certain words in class. This may seem inconsequential to those observing, but what if this leads the child with the speech impairment to drop out of school?

The child doing the teasing and the adult who witnesses the behavior may not feel that they are doing anything wrong, but what's important is not what those with power feel. The important thing is to understand how the excluded feel and *why* they feel that way.

All of us have been excluded at some point, and it never feels good. But while being left out of a trip to the movies by your family feels terrible in the moment, it is different from the most pernicious and hard-to-combat kinds of exclusion: those that are structural or institutional, and that transcend a singular context or experience. These are the kinds of exclusions that people refer to as "systemic."

Racism, tribalism, sexism, and the many other negative "-isms" are all examples. When we directly observe individuals enforcing these exclusions verbally or physically, I would hope that we would stop and intervene. But people are excluded from all sorts of activities and opportunities every day.

Many of us remain silent even if we're disturbed by it, and the world goes on. That's why the first step to enhancing inclusion is to identify the things that lead people to feel excluded, at both an individual and a systemic level, and put a name to them. Once we name something, it is harder to ignore.

Before he named me education minister, President Bio and I had spoken informally about the ban on pregnant girls in schools a few times, both over lunch at his office and also casually at his home. He knew my position clearly and though he hadn't said as much explicitly, my sense from our conversations was that he was open to reviewing the ban. When my mind tuned back in to the president's voice in the conference center, everything he was saying was music to my ears. He spoke about the government's flagship Free Quality School Education program which was enrolling more and more learners across the nation, including increasing numbers of girls. Then he lifted his head ever so slightly and looked up at the high wooden ceilings of the auditorium, which were swathed with cobwebs. He seemed to be pondering a question. I had already spent enough time around the president to learn some of his mannerisms. I could tell he was about to go off script because he placed his left index finger on a line on the paper as a marker.

I knew he was pondering something important; I did not know what. Then he spoke. "People have asked me if pregnant schoolgirls should go to school," he began. I squirmed uneasily in my seat.

He took a pause, which felt like eternity.

Could he have seen the same girl I saw on his way to this event? Why was he bringing up this topic at this time? For a brief moment, I got excited, hoping he would seize the occasion to overturn the ban right there and then. But it quickly passed.

"For me, I say no," he said, going straight to the point. "If a girl child is pregnant, let her stay home until she delivers before she can return to school."

The president looked directly at me as he spoke, catching and holding my gaze briefly before he lowered his eyes. As he further expanded his thoughts, looking in the direction of where the development partners and diplomats were sitting, I sank deeper and deeper into my chair. It felt to me like the world had stopped spinning; gravity had ceased to exist, and I was just floating in that auditorium. All of a sudden, I was a key part of a government that was actively supporting a policy that I found deeply objectionable but would be tasked to enforce. There was absolutely no ambiguity in the president's position.

I wasn't sure what was more shocking—the president's words or the loud applause that followed. One of the promises of our government was it would be different from its predecessors in matters of what we refer to as "human capital development." Gender equity and access to education are central to human capital development. Why did the president not see that his policy was exclusionary, in conflict with human capital development, and a continuation of the previous government's bad policy? Why did he not just stick to his script?

Before I wandered off in worried thought for too long, I was jolted back to reality by the loud clapping of the young girl who was sitting right next to me. She looked at me with glee as she said, "Maada Bio is right. I do not want to be in the same classroom as a pregnant girl." She did not know who I was, and I had not asked for her opinion, but she felt it was important to express her support for what the president had just said.

She must have seen from my expression that I did not agree. I took a deep breath and asked her to tell me why she felt the president was right. I listened attentively for a while as she repeated the same points that lobbying groups had been pushing for the past decade: pregnant girls need to be protected; they are bad influences on their peers in the classroom; it isn't morally right; allowing them to attend school is tantamount to condoning sexual activity among teenage girls. And that was just for starters. After listening for a long while, I cut her off mid-sentence. "It is OK, thank you," I said.

I'd had enough, and I had not even completed a full day in my job as minister.

Many people had opposed my appointment. During my parliamentary approval interviews, I responded to a critique from a member of Parliament who had said I was an inexperienced politician who wouldn't last in the post. He was right about my political inexperience, I told him, but I was there "to do my job, not to keep my job." Now I wondered whether his critique was justified and whether I was even ready to do the job.

When I accepted President Bio's generous invitation to join his cabinet, some civil society organizations and social activists had rightly assumed that overturning the ban would be one of my top goals. But in that auditorium, for the first time in my life, I began to wonder if something I had set my mind to might prove impossible to accomplish. Surely if the president, as head of government and head of cabinet, publicly stated his view on something, then that was the policy that everyone else on the team should support. I considered resigning, but not for long. Holding a view that pregnant girls should not go to school did not make that girl who sat next to me in the auditorium or President Bio, or anyone else who held the same view, a bad person. Many who were against pregnant girls going to school just didn't realize how exclusionary the policy was. But if the image of that girl in the street had refocused my attention, the president had drawn the battle lines in the most public way. And I was ready to fight.

To my mind, the issue was crystal clear and unambiguous. Every child has an inalienable right to a quality education, no matter their condition. That our society had accepted that a female child could lose this right was unjust. It took a boy and a girl for a girl to become pregnant, but the pregnancy was, of course, borne solely by the girl. That girl crossing the street should have been on her way to a school compound that morning and yet, because she was pregnant, she was out in the streets going anywhere except a school. That was not right.

Civil society activists and feminist organizations had been fighting against the ban for nearly half a decade. But an even louder set of activists believed, just as the schoolgirl sitting next to me did, that allowing pregnant girls into classrooms would set a bad example for young people. Now that I was squarely in the middle of the conflict, I made a commitment to delve deeper into both sides' positions so I could build my own arguments more effectively.

Before I walked out of that auditorium, I vowed to make overturning the ban not just one of my top goals, but the very top one. Education—safe access to schools, retention in class, transition to higher grades, quality of learning—is not always equitable for boys and girls in Sierra Leone, nor is it in many countries. Girls are systematically excluded through explicit policies, institutional infrastructure, and sociocultural practices. This is further exacerbated by sexual and gender-based violence. I did not know how to solve all those problems, but I knew it was unjust to deprive pregnant girls of their education. That, at least, was something we should and could remedy.

The first step, I realized, was to name this exclusion loudly, clearly, and without equivocation. But I also knew that the voices that needed to be centered in the conversation were those of the people who were being left out. Over the years, I'd heard all sorts of people opine on this topic—from older women to schoolgirls, from religious leaders to cultural leaders and government officials—but seldom had I heard from a schoolgirl who had actually been barred from school because she was pregnant.

The full weight of the first principle of radical inclusion hit me in that moment like a log over my head. I had been feeling sorry for the pregnant girl I saw on my way to the auditorium. But there's a huge difference between feeling sympathy for someone and identifying an exclusion in a way that accurately reflects its true reality. No exclusion can be remedied until you research it, gain a deep understanding of its complexities, and then define it in a way that makes its injustice unambiguously clear to others. So, how many pregnant schoolgirls had I talked to myself? The answer was exactly none.

As I concluded recounting my day to Kate, I promised myself that I would meet as many people affected by the ban as I could. And I did. Starting the very next morning, I actively sought out pregnant schoolgirls and parent learners (meaning someone who had a child and returned to school). I listened as they told me that while there were indeed some physical challenges related to school attendance, there was absolutely nothing that significantly affected their ability to learn. One girl told me that whether she was in school or not, the morning sickness and nausea were the same. She would rather be in school with morning sickness than suffer through it while selling peanuts in front of her house. The teenage mothers who had just recently given birth reported being taunted by both their teachers and their classmates, especially when they opted out of certain activities. Many chose to stay home rather than subject themselves to the constant shaming and bullying in school.

The pregnant girls and parent learners told me about other ways their exclusion from the classroom affected them. At home they were pressured to either get married or do more household labor, taking them further away from their educations. Friends from school shunned them, sometimes because they no longer shared the same interests but also because their parents forced them to end their friendships with girls who were pregnant. While their pregnancies took a toll on their bodies, the psychological and psychosocial challenges were equally arduous. Many suffered from depression.

One thing I never heard from any of them was that they had become pregnant because they saw that another girl in their school was pregnant. So it seemed hard to imagine how their presence in a classroom would result in other girls deciding to become pregnant.

One weekend in early 2020, I went to visit my mother in Bo. My parents' compound is always filled with members of our extended family who are either visiting or found reasons to stay on. Our compound also has a clean water well with a tap. Ever since I was a kid, several other families in the neighborhood have used that well as their source of drinking water. Neighborhood schoolchildren go there during their lunch breaks to get water as well, so on any given day, between fifty and a hundred children come to get water for their families.

Lucky for me, a young pregnant girl came to fetch some drinking water as I rested under a coconut tree in the yard. She had a *lappa* wrapped around her torso, and walking behind her and kicking a small football was a boy I assumed to be her younger brother. I asked if she wanted to join me for a conversation. She agreed and we walked to the veranda, which offered more privacy than the well.

I'll call her Aminata. While she did not reveal who the father of her child was (I did not ask), she pointedly observed that he was still doing what he did before she became pregnant, which was going to school; only she was being punished by the state.

But when I asked Aminata if she wished she could attend school during her pregnancy, her answer was vehement: "No!" When she saw how surprised I was, she explained that while she wanted to continue her education, it was difficult for her to concentrate because of morning sickness. It had been the same with her first pregnancy, she said, explaining that the little boy who accompanied her to the well was not her younger brother but her son, delivered just after she completed junior secondary school, likely before her sixteenth birthday.

Aminata came from Pujehun District, which has one of the highest teenage pregnancy rates in Sierra Leone. Many of her other classmates either have children already or are pregnant. Several hid their pregnancies from their families and teachers until they could no longer do so. She had done that herself with her first child, which was how she was able to take her junior secondary school examination. This was more difficult to do in some schools, where, as a pregnancy check, teachers would reportedly measure the size of girls' bellies as they stood in line to take exams. But she could not hide her pregnancy this time because her uniform was too tight. What made her situation worse was that the government policy didn't just forbid her to attend school; it also forbade her from registering to take the national exam to continue her education.

Aminata burst into tears as she grappled with the prospect of missing a whole school year. With two babies, she might never be able to go back. I could not give her any comfort as I fought to hold back my own tears. How is it that we as a society are so good at further victimizing those who are already victims? Twelve years of public education and she was at risk of not graduating from secondary school. Twelve years of public investment in her education and now the state was limiting her potential. Why? Aminata left with a full bucket of fresh, clean water balanced on her head, as her son kicked his ball behind her.

I got back to Freetown in time for dinner. As I sat down in front of my plate of rice and fish stew, I couldn't keep my thoughts to myself. "I have a question, everyone," I blurted out. "Do you think pregnant girls should be allowed to attend school with non-pregnant girls?"

The table was silent. I didn't expect Nyaanina to have an opinion; while she was an avid debater with a lot to say about most things, she wasn't going to have any thoughts on this topic; she was, after all, only four at the time. But I was surprised to hear nothing from her cousin. After a minute or so, I directed the question explicitly to Kadija. "What do you think?" I asked. She thought for a bit and then she murmured, "No."

I felt a gagging sensation in my throat and reached for a glass of water to wash it down. If I had still been drinking alcohol, I would have taken a sip from Kate's glass of wine. But since our dinner table is a safe space where we reason and debate without judgment, I asked Kadija to explain why she felt that way. "I don't know," she replied.

"I don't know" is the answer Kadija gives when she doesn't want to engage on a particular topic. Part of the reason I was shocked is because Kadija is a child who always looks after others. As just one example, she's a loving big sister to Peynina and Nyaanina. They spend hours together learning how to sing new Afrobeat songs and practicing their dance moves. On special occasions they often wear the same dresses and hairstyles.

I really wanted to know, and I wanted her to feel free to tell me what she honestly thought. "Why do you think you might feel that way?" I pressed her. She rattled through a few thoughts, leading with the classic "They will set a bad example for other students." Her spoon clanged against her white IKEA dish as she took another bite of her dinner.

I waited for a while, and then I asked her if she thought she might want to get pregnant if she sat next to a pregnant girl. Her response was quick, almost automatic. "No. But what about the other girls?" I recognized her concern, but I told her she should trust them to make good decisions, just as she trusted herself to. If the answer was "no" for her, why couldn't it be "no" for them as well? She paused, took another big spoonful of stew, and looked away. I didn't want to press the issue and Kate sensed the tension. Changing the subject, she asked me about my trip to Bo.

Instead of feeling frustrated with Kadija, who was simply being honest, I realized I needed to do a better job of identifying and defining the exclusion so I could help others understand its injustice. What was obvious to me wasn't obvious to them, and I wasn't doing a good job of explaining myself. If I was to convince the president, his cabinet, and the country, including members of my own family, I needed to have both quantitative and qualitative data. I committed to having more conversations with girls who looked like Aminata and Kadija.

The more I worked to identify this specific exclusion, the more I learned about the toll it was taking, and not just on the girls, but on society at large. Sierra Leone's literacy rate is less than 40 percent overall, and less than 10 percent for adult rural women. The odds that a rural girl will complete secondary school are orders of magnitude worse than those for an urban boy. Research clearly shows that every additional year of secondary education that a mother completes has a direct and positive correlation on her family's income and her children's health. And keeping pregnant girls out of school wasn't making them any safer; teenage pregnancies account for nearly half of Sierra Leone's high maternal mortality rate.

In my role as a minister, I was responsible for programs that directly touched millions of children and over eighty thousand teachers in nearly every village in the country. My priority was to support the president's vision of universal and equitable access to education, with the emphasis on *universal*. But the more I engaged the president, the cabinet, and others on the topic of pregnant girls attending school, the more alone I felt. I was continually reminded that my views were outside the norm.

It wasn't enough to identify the problem if people didn't see it as a problem; I needed to summon the data, share the stories behind the numbers, and, more than that, convey the psychological impact. I thought back to times in my life when I had felt excluded. There had been several recent instances when colleagues made me feel excluded, even though I am one of the most senior members of government. At a small gathering with the president and a handful of ministers, one of them referred to me as a *pumuin*—a Mende word that translates literally to "foreign person" but is also used to mean "white person" or "stranger." Other colleagues have made it a point to observe that I dress, eat (I am a pescatarian, which is odd in Sierra Leone), and often behave differently than Sierra Leoneans are expected to.

However, I also drew strength from a powerful instance of inclusion in which someone had brought me from the margin to the center—and not just any person, but the president. It was during a hectic road trip in rural Sierra Leone. Tired from a long day of community engagements, seven of us, six ministers and a parliamentarian, were sitting with the president when he asked one of us to find someone who wasn't present and ask him to join us. I quickly volunteered. The parliamentarian, following protocol, suggested that it was he who should do this task rather than me because I had the more senior position. I insisted it was no problem, and continued on my way. I should add that I was also the youngest person in the room, and I felt obliged or perhaps expected to run such errands, because our culture accords a great deal of respect to elders.

When I returned, the parliamentarian said, "Honorable Minister, I want to tell you what the president said after you left. He called you an 'unconventional minister.'" I don't think the parliamentarian understood the power that the president's words held for me, but it was in that moment that I felt most "seen" and "understood" in my role in the government. I was unconventional. And it wasn't just in that instance. Whenever I felt most excluded by others within the system, the person who always brought me back into the center was the one who held the most power and whose opinion mattered the most: the president. That was why I felt I had a chance at doing my job, even if many of the stakeholders in the system did not support me originally. When it was most important, I felt seen. That was also why I believed that there was hope that we would be able to overturn the ban and allow pregnant girls to pursue their dreams.

That's what gave me my strategy and my most crucial guiding principle. I needed to make sure that the girls themselves felt like they were being seen. Only then could they believe that change was possible. If the effort was going to be for them, it also had to be *by* them.

I should have realized this right from the start. But the importance of it occurred to me only when I thought back further, not just to the kind of exclusion I felt when I left home to travel abroad, or to the things I had experienced in my cabinet role, but to my earliest memories as a primary school kid. The full import of it came to me only after I thought back to times when I had been the *excluder* and not the *excluded*. It was painful but paramount for me to look at the times in my life when I had been responsible for keeping others on the margin, not out of deliberate cruelty but simply because I hadn't bothered to look around me or consider anyone but myself.

To fully appreciate why people must be seen for change to happen, I had to grapple with the times when it was I who hadn't noticed people who desperately wanted to be seen. The irony, and it's not lost on me, is that I didn't even realize what I hadn't seen until one of my childhood friends pointed it out when we were reminiscing about our earliest days in Bo.

As my friend reminded me, every evening, about an hour before sunset, a dozen or so of us boys would gather in the middle of a brown dirt field beside the Bo-Kenema Highway to play football (or soccer, as it is known in North America). This was in the mid-1990s, and we were all between the ages of eight and fifteen. Some of us were always barefoot, and others owned flat rubber sandals, ironically called *stilettos* in Krio, the local dialect. A few had proper shoes, but none of this mattered as we anxiously listened for our names to be called out.

"I pick Jinnah," one of the designated leaders for that day would shout (the names in this story have been changed). Jinnah, a short boy with radiant dark skin and slightly bowed legs, wore neon green shoes, and he walked with the confidence and sense of purpose that went with the knowledge that his name would always be called first or second. We all wanted to be like him. "Mohamed, come," another of the captains would respond. One by one, we would excitedly line up behind the two captains.

Only at the very end would they call Mustapha's and Saidu's names; those boys were always picked last, and only to complete or balance the team numbers. Everyone knew that, and most important, the unspoken rules were that those who were picked last had no choice in what position they played; they were always the goalkeepers. Zidane, Ronaldo, Okocha, Owen, and all the other global football stars we admired were not goalkeepers, a position no boy would ever choose to play.

When he was finally called, Mustapha would sluggishly march toward his team. He was no Jinnah, but he didn't care. Football was much more than just fun for us; it was life, and everyone wanted to play the beautiful game. Rain or shine, we were ready to play well past sunset until we could hardly see the ball. It was very clear to all of us in that bubble of neighborhood friends that the only factor that went into our selection was skill. Or that's what we told ourselves.

But our bubble wasn't perfect after all. There were kids we never invited to play. We excluded them so completely that we never even realized it. All it took was one simple action by one kid to open our eyes and radically change our perspective.

One day, a player got injured during a tightly contested match. The captain of the team that was now one player short—a new kid whose family had recently relocated to the police barracks opposite the football field—shouted without thinking (or so we all must have thought), "Bakarr, come stand in goal for us. Mustapha will play in defense."

Bakarr was a sweet boy who had been coming to the field nearly every evening. At first he had stood in the middle of the field with the rest of us, but not once was his name called. No one even noticed when he moved to the sidelines and became a permanent spectator. That's just what he was, a spectator. If someone got tired or injured and there was no one else to pick from, we played with unequal teams instead of inviting Bakarr to join us. He wasn't excluded because he was hated; he was our friend and we did everything else together: eat, study, and watch football matches on TV. No, the reason we never picked him was that he lived with a disability. His left leg was partially paralyzed as a result of childhood polio. As such, no one even considered including him in our daily games. We wanted to win so badly that we figured we were better off one player down than having Bakarr on our teams.

Everyone was so shocked when this new kid called Bakarr, including Bakarr himself, that it took a whole minute before any of us understood what was happening. "Bakarr, come on, please, we have to win this game. We don't have much time before it turns into night," he shouted impatiently. Bakarr limped across the field and stood valiantly in goal, a broad disbelieving smile on his face, and the game continued on as if nothing had happened. Everyone on the field quickly refocused their attention to the ball.

I don't remember the outcome of the match—it certainly didn't matter—but soon after we left the field, and for long periods after that, no one could stop talking about Bakarr's performance; he had made some terrific saves. Before long, Bakarr was joining us in the middle of the field again as well, waiting for his name to be called alongside Jinnah's, Mohamed's, and mine. Even though he was an excellent goalkeeper, he wasn't only called for goalie. He felt seen. As the games got more intense, goalkeeping became more important, and goalkeepers were no longer chosen last. Everyone, including Mustapha and Saidu, was now picked with the expectation that they would contribute with their skills to helping their teams win. Our fun game became even more beautiful when we removed the barriers of exclusion such that everyone who wanted to play could be picked, and not always last.

It took a new kid to make me realize that I wasn't a passive observer; I had been an excluder, and our games and lives had been the poorer for it.

Now that I'm an adult, I know that I need to model inclusive behavior for my children, even as I work to dismantle the underlying structures that reinforce exclusion. Those structures are often complex. As it happened, Bakarr was perfectly able to compete; we just hadn't given him the opportunity.

Even he had begun to assume he couldn't. But how do we enhance the play or socialization of children with physical disabilities who may require some form of accommodation? When we throw birthday parties for our children, we often choose to organize football games and provide bouncing castles and trampolines. But when we do so, do we notice the child with crutches who is sitting in the corner? Do we notice when such children eventually stop showing up to birthday parties because they feel excluded? When we invite our daughters' friends to a pool or beach party, do we provide alternative activities for their hijab-wearing classmates, or those who do not know how to swim?

To notice and remedy instances of exclusion, we need to be intentional in looking for them by asking several questions: Are there groups of people who are missing at the table? It could be because of where the table is, its height, the food we are serving at it, what was said in the invitation, or how the invitation itself was sent. Whatever the reasons, the first step in identifying an exclusion is to find out who is missing. Who is not seen?

Once we see the pattern, the next step is to acknowledge it. Acknowledging, naming, and identifying such exclusions can be extremely difficult and even embarrassing for us. I'm still ashamed when I think of Bakarr, our friend, spending so many games on the sidelines. And worse, it hadn't even occurred to me that we never invited any girls to play with us. Girls were supposed to be at home, doing chores or skipping rope. Unlike Bakarr, who was on the margin, girls were not even in our universe. This kind of shame can lead to two things: It can lead us to close our minds and deny that the exclusion exists as we tell ourselves that *those people* could have joined the circle if they had wanted to, or if they had worked just a little harder. Or it can spur us to make a commitment to change the situation.

The naming or acknowledgment has to first be personal—it begins with each of us—but ultimately it has to be public as well, and loud enough that those who are excluded can hear it. That public acknowledgment can take several forms, including opinion articles in newspapers, discussions at school debate competitions, or via the creation of organizations of like-minded people who champion the cause of inclusion. It must not just include but be *centered* on the people most affected. "Nothing for us without us" is the motto of many groups who have traditionally been sidelined and aren't willing to be passive spectators as others swoop in to try to fix things for them.

And then we come back to facts. The data and references you present when advocating for more inclusive communities must be accepted and recognized by anyone who is reasonably open to new perspectives. But to convince others means that all perspectives must be fully captured. Evidence is a powerful thing, but a flaw in the data can bring everything crashing down, no matter how sound your argument and how thorough your research. Once someone notices that flaw, their minds may snap shut. The data should also cover as many different contexts as possible, starting locally and going globally.

When I first started discussing the ban, I did it everywhere. I did it over lunch with the president; I discussed it during subcommittee meetings; I spoke to journalists on the radio about it; and I would ask people for their thoughts about it in their homes, in schools, and at the workplace. Essentially, everywhere I went, I sought to hear the full spectrum of opinions. I wanted to hear for myself if others could see the exclusion the way I did. If we couldn't agree on what it was and its extent and ill effects, then how could we possibly begin to talk about the need for change?

Seven-year-old Amina is the president's youngest daughter, and she and Nyaanina were classmates in the first grade. The president and I often bring up our daughters as we discuss and think through government policies. We both want to have a Sierra Leone where our children can grow up to be confident that they can fulfill their human potential. To that end, we want to ensure they receive the fundamentals. First, and most critical, is a quality education, in which they learn all the skills necessary to fully participate in a globally competitive world.

While President Bio and I had starkly different views on the ban, still, I felt fully supported by him in all other aspects of my work. I knew that if I didn't succeed in changing his mind, I would have no one to blame but myself. I had the resources, the mandate, and the time to engage on the topic, which I believed was critically important for my daughters and all the girls of Sierra Leone. It was up to me to do so, despite his very public disagreement.

After that World Children's Day event, I returned to the State House, where I joined the president for lunch. I waited for the perfect time to engage on the topic, hoping he would clarify his thinking. But even before I finished asking him why he'd said what he did, the other two guests at the dining table interrupted to say that the president had spoken well. When he reaffirmed his position, I stopped tasting my food. But then he added that he had never seen a pregnant girl in school himself, or spoken to one who wanted to be in school. Growing up, he said, he knew stories of girls getting pregnant, but they'd all stayed at home. He added that he might be willing to change his mind if he heard from a pregnant girl who had gone to school, or if he was convinced by evidence that her presence would have no ill effects on her classmates. I advanced to the dessert and smiled, because I knew there was a small sliver of hope.

2

Listen, to Understand and Learn

· · · · ·

Empathy is a strange and powerful thing. There is no script. There is no right way or wrong way to do it. There is simply listening, holding space, withholding judgment, emotionally connecting, and communicating that incredibly healing message of "You're not alone."

—BRENÉ BROWN

Once you've identified and named an exclusion, you've made an important first step forward. Not just important, but crucial; you can't start to fix a problem until you accept its existence. So, you can pat yourself on the back for that. But we all know about lots of problems in our families, our organizations, our nations, and our world without having any real understanding of them. We can google to our hearts' content, but still not know much or understand more.

Where do we start?

The problem is that we can't fix a problem until we know its scope. Einstein, one of the world's greatest modern thinkers, captured this well when he said that if he only had an hour to solve a problem he'd spend fifty-five minutes thinking about the problem and only five minutes thinking about the solution.

On the inclusion of pregnant girls in school, I realized quickly that I had a lot of learning ahead of me and that I was going to have to talk to—and most important, listen to—all sorts of people before I could figure out next steps. This included those who were strongly invested in keeping the ban in place and those who did not care or were not directly affected.

The Bombali District Council Office is right off the main highway connecting Makeni, our fourth-largest city with a population of just over one hundred thousand, to Freetown, which is not just our capital but also our largest city. Sierra Leone has sixteen districts, and each has its own council office building that contains large open halls for meetings. I had been to many of these halls, but this was my first time in the Bombali District Council. As soon as I arrived, I was guided toward a table on a high concrete platform surrounded by brightly colored plastic chairs, all of them vacant. Even though I was up there by myself, any feeling of loneliness quickly evaporated when I sat down in a pink chair and looked at the audience. The hall was packed.

I recognized a few of the faces in the room from my last visit to Makeni, which had been to commission some new schools the government had built. I was a little concerned that I didn't know more of the attendees, as they were all educators and hence employees of my ministry, but I was heartened to see that there were a lot more women than men, given the issue I intended to raise. The room was vibrant with the batik, kente, and cotton print fabrics they wore. They matched the colorful-print shirt I was wearing, and I felt like I blended right in.

But I was still nervous. I avoided making eye contact with anyone for fear they could read my thoughts. The overhead fan immediately above me was not working; my sweat stuck my shirt to my body. I used the book I had as a hand fan, waving it from left to right, as I waited for the meeting to begin.

Though it was still bright outside, the clock on the wall read 5:57 P.M. Because of the local sociocultural phenomenon known as "Salone time" ("Salone" is the Krio nickname for Sierra Leone), most people arrive at town hall meetings late and they rarely start on time. Not in that hall, and not on that day. I was told the room had filled up half an hour earlier. The moment the minute hand hit the twelve, the mics were turned on.

The deputy director of education, who is in charge of all matters relating to education in the district, began: "Mr. Minister, over one hundred heads of schools, principals, senior teachers, and executive members of the Sierra Leone Teachers Union, Conference of Principals, and National Council of Head Teachers, among other institutions from all over Makeni, have honored your invitation to this town hall meeting. Although I sent the notice only a couple of hours ago, as you can see, Mr. Minister, the turnout has been overwhelming."

Even with the feedback from the crude PA system and the loud motors of the overhead fans that did work, the quaver in the director's voice came through clearly. He is normally a confident man with a commanding presence, but he was visibly nervous. I sensed that he wasn't sure why so many people had turned up and was anxious about what might happen, given that there were no items on my agenda other than an open discussion on education matters. Passing the microphone to me, he returned to his seat in the audience.

His nervousness was understandable, given the fraught politics of Sierra Leone. The country's sixteen districts are geographically clustered into five regions. Bombali is in the northern region, which, along with the northwest region, is a stronghold of the All People's Congress (APC), one of Sierra Leone's two major political parties. The other is the Sierra Leone People's Party (SLPP), whose strongholds are in the southern and eastern regions (the western region is evenly divided between the two parties). Excepting several military juntas that briefly seized power after coups, one or the other of those parties has governed the country continuously since April 27, 1961, when we gained our independence from Great Britain.

In recent history, between 1996 and 2007, Sierra Leone was governed by the SLPP and then, between 2007 and 2018, by the APC. After a tightly contested free and fair election that went into a runoff in 2018, the SLPP emerged victorious and returned to power. His Excellency President Julius Maada Bio established his New Direction government after that April 2018 victory.

These political divides are exacerbated by Sierra Leone's tribal and ethnic divides. The predominant ethnicity in the South and East is Mende, while in the North it's Temne. The languages the Mende and Temne speak are linguistically distinct, and very few people speak both. English is Sierra Leone's official language and Krio its lingua franca. But the Mende and Temne account for more than two-thirds of the country's population, and the tensions between them are always heightened during and after elections.

That is why my staff had urged me not to when I told them I wanted to schedule this impromptu town hall in a stronghold of the opposition APC. They feared partisans would seek to disrupt the meeting. But that was exactly why I had chosen Bombali for this event. I didn't want a friendly, hometown crowd. I wanted an opportunity to listen to, under-stand, and respond to people who may not even want us to succeed—who were likely to be hostile to the government and, by extension, to me and my ideas.

One of the ministerial activities I enjoy the most is holding informal small group meetings, where people make jokes, dis-cuss difficult issues, and then at the end give each other smiles and high fives. Although someone may ask about something you don't have an answer to, you can still let them know you heard them by acknowledging their fears and concerns.

There's a big difference, however, between small group meetings in an office and town halls, especially in areas that don't reflect your political base. Politicians do not typically enjoy town hall meetings because they can get sticky quickly. Though perhaps I should add that there are some rare politi-cians who actually do enjoy them—President Bio and former US president Barack Obama among them. They listen, do not claim to know the answers to everything, and deploy humor in their responses even to "unfair" questions. I'd learned a lot from both of them and was determined to channel their energies on this occasion.

When I took the microphone from the deputy director, I realized how tired I was. I had been on the road for days and traveled great distances to other districts. But the minute I opened my mouth, my energy level surged. I was struck by what a gift it was to have so many passionate people in front of me, eager to share what was on their minds. I thanked them for coming and reiterated that I wanted their unbounded and unconstrained opinions. They looked surprised and maybe a little skeptical, but I truly meant it.

To address some of the biggest elephants in the room, I started by saying that I had noticed how many of them were holding notes, and that I had a good idea of the kinds of issues they wanted to bring up. They weren't hard to guess. The critical national issues that were of most concern to teachers and education administrators were the large numbers of volunteer and community teachers who were not employed directly by the government, the late payments of government subsidies, and the need for additional furniture and classrooms. I assured them that we were working on all of them and gave concrete timelines for their resolutions. The energy in the room settled a bit as more and more heads nodded in agreement. As I discussed other policies that the government had either implemented or was considering, I noticed some of the attendees returning their notes to their bags and pockets. I assumed this was because I had addressed their issues. Then, while running through a list of initiatives, I mentioned my desire to do away with the ban on pregnant girls in schools. I purposefully included it in a list to see if it would stand out.

It did. The mood in the room instantly changed, and

greatly for the worse. I didn't dwell on reversing the ban but spoke about it in a matter-of-fact tone, and said just enough about it to spur a general discussion. Still, the effect was dramatic.

When I invited comments and questions from the audience, many hands shot up. Speaking over the sharp horns of the *kekeh* tricycles on the highway outside, transporting people home at the end of their workdays, I responded to each question and comment in general, noncommittal ways, so as not to shut out more feedback. Even so, resistance to lifting the ban on pregnant girls was seemingly universal. Several teachers and principals expressed concern about the impact this would have in their schools. My goal had been to hear as many arguments against changing the policy as possible, and I did. In fact, it seemed like the more people discussed the idea, the more emboldened they became in their opposition. I had resolved to listen and empathize, but I knew I also had to make an effort to dispel some of the myths and misinformation I was hearing.

I noticed that one of the women in the room had attempted to raise her hand several times, but her elbow never quite straightened, and her hand never passed above her ears. I knew she had something to say but was either shy or not sure how the room would react. I'd not called on her earlier so as not to put her on the spot. In the end, though, I decided that she really did seem to want to speak, so as the meeting was about to wrap up, I called on her. "Yes, madam," I said. "You in the back wearing that beautiful orange dress, it seems like you have something you want to share." I also admit to harboring the hope that she would have something positive to say.

Her head wrap had the same bright orange pattern as her dress. She stood up slowly, flashing a gentle smile as she took the microphone, shuffling awkwardly as she screwed up her nerve to speak. It was the end of a long day and a long, contentious session, but as soon as she started talking, a golden silence fell upon that hot and humid hall. She radiated an air of calm that made us all feel more comfortable.

"Gloria," she began. "My name is Gloria, and I am the principal of a UMC junior secondary school here in Makeni." She paused for a breath, and then said that she wanted to talk about the policy the government was thinking of institutionalizing that would allow pregnant girls back in school. First, she asked me what the government planned to do to protect and serve the pregnant girls and parent learners upon their return. I told her that I would answer, of course, but wondered if she would be willing to continue expressing her thoughts. She nodded and continued. In rural communities, she explained, parents often kick their pregnant teenagers out of their homes, saying that they can't afford to feed a teenager and a newborn baby at the same time. Pregnancy signified adulthood and they felt they shouldn't have to provide for an adult.

Gloria then revealed that she herself had become pregnant when she was fifteen, at the end of her final year in junior secondary school. Heads turned and eyes widened as the other school principals and leaders took in her words. Gloria has a big presence; she carries herself so majestically that I am guessing that no one there could have imagined her as a pregnant schoolgirl. There was no shame in her voice, but you could hear some discomfort as she shared her story—perhaps for the first time in public. In fact, it was the first time I'd heard anyone share such a story in public.

Gloria said that she had been taken into a private welfare home in Port Loko after her family stopped supporting her. It had not been easy for her to cope with her pregnancy, her loss of schooling, and the further victimization she experienced from the community. She concluded by stating that even though she was very happy with the proposed policy change, she was unsure about its implementation, because it could not succeed without community engagement at the family and household level, and I had not discussed that in my presentation.

As Gloria recounted her own ordeal, I saw the emotions on people's faces change. In that moment, it became clear to me that the most powerful tool for changing deeply entrenched perspectives is empathy. Nothing I could have said would have left the same impression on the hearts and minds of the teachers than what Gloria shared. She was one of them; she channeled something I didn't have and represented something I wasn't and would never be.

As Gloria spoke, I looked over at one of the male teachers who had spoken up in support of the ban. It was remarkable to watch his surprise turn into resignation, and then evolve into warm approval. He nodded his head gently, unclenched his hands, and wrote something down on the paper he was holding as Gloria spoke about how she uses her own experience to engage the parents of pregnant girls, urging them to give their daughters the support they need so they can continue to learn. Listening to Gloria, the school leaders were learning something I could never have taught them.

At the end of the meeting, I asked my assistant Grace to get Gloria's phone number so we could continue our conversation and maybe even figure out how to work together. In telling her story, Gloria had moved from being a silent observer to an activist. As an activist, she was now challenging others to see and hear what she felt, both when she was fifteen and today. She was able to evoke empathy in her colleagues because of her honesty and eloquence, but also because she could at one and the same time speak from the perspective of a pregnant schoolgirl, a school administrator, and a community member who was doing something many had thought impossible: educating pregnant girls and making sure they were properly supported.

Her words and presence provided a sobering thought that was also a challenge. Gloria was now a principal and head of a school, even though she'd once been a pregnant schoolgirl. But how many other potential Glorias were being lost because of our failure to see and hear them, and the institutional barriers we placed in their paths? It was a question I'm sure everyone else was pondering as the meeting ended. The other question, of course, was how much were we as a society losing by robbing ourselves of the talents of so many people like Gloria?

Grace was not the only one trying to get Gloria's attention after the meeting. Some of her colleagues had circled around her, and they were now discussing the issue in clearer terms and with much more nuance. This was a significant moment for me because, as you will recall, we were in an area where the population was, for political reasons, largely opposed to the ideas of the central government. If the inclusion of pregnant girls in schools was to be successful, it would need to be supported by people from both political parties and every region. When I first began speaking about the topic publicly, criticism and support had formed along party lines. The goal of this town hall had been to change that, and Gloria had given me the hope and the confidence to continue reaching out to those who were likely to oppose our ideas. It was an opportunity to learn and potentially get those opponents on our side as advocates. But that was not even the biggest lesson I learned that day.

Gloria had started by asking about the support the government would provide to families and communities if the policy change took place. Her question made me realize that the target population was not just the pregnant girls and their schools but their family units at home. Gloria challenged me and everyone else in the room to take a 360-degree view of the problem. For once, it seemed we were all on the same page.

Here's the thing. If conversations are hard, then meaningful conversations about hard things seem impossible. But lucky for us, there is plenty of research out there that helps us have them. Harvard University's Robert Livingston addresses the importance of collectively understanding a problem in its full scope in his book *The Conversation* (which I recommend you read, as it offers a rich and practical approach to talking about really difficult topics). Before we can solve a problem, Dr. Livingston writes, we must agree on what the problem is, who it affects, what makes it a problem, and so on. His work focuses on racism, which is an obvious and widely recognized form of exclusion, but it is applicable—perhaps even more so—to other forms of exclusion, the consequences of which are not seen, such as banning pregnant girls from attending school.

I left that town hall with a renewed appreciation for the power of empathetic listening. Empathy is not always easy to access, especially when you are introducing new ideas to people who are already opposed to most of what you have to say on principle. The easiest way to bridge those differences is to have someone from within the group challenge its assumptions. Gloria was our bridge in this instance, and whether she knew it or not, she had become part of our team. Whatever policy document my ministry developed would have to include more than the girls directly affected by the ban—it would have to include the broader communities they belonged to as well.

The next day, I traveled to Kono District in the eastern region, accompanied by Madam Emily Kadiatu Gogra, the deputy minister of basic and senior secondary education. Madam Gogra and I complement each other well. Although we are both members of the same political party, she's from the North and I come from the South. She is Temne and I am Mende. She served for many years as a teacher and proprietor of a school when I was still in school; like many of the people I work with, she's old enough to be my mother. Though she is the first to point out that she used to be afraid of technology, she is curious about it and loves learning from young people, relying on her grandchildren to teach her about the functions and apps on her phone. I hold several patents and my love for technology is an open secret. I am often referred to as the technocrat and Madam Gogra as the grassroots politician.

As we sat in a dusty school compound waiting to speak, I told Madam Gogra about what happened at the meeting in Makeni the day before. Before I even mentioned Gloria's name, I saw that she was smiling and had something to say. "Gloria is one of my kids," she told me. It turns out that the private welfare home in Port Loko that had taken Gloria in belonged to Madam Gogra. The home takes care of pregnant girls and then sends them to school as parent learners after they've delivered their babies. The babies are provided with daycare and early education. Madam Gogra's welfare home also engages the parents of the pregnant girls, and has often succeeded in reintegrating them with their families, which is what happened with Gloria.

Although the deputy minister and I work closely together, I was surprised and intrigued to learn this about her. Then a young woman stopped by to say hello to Madam Gogra, interrupting our conversation. She was introduced to me as a teacher at the school, but I did not catch her name. After she left, Madam Gogra told me that she had also been one of her girls in Port Loko. Though I worked closely with Madam Gogra, I had never talked with her at such length outside of a meeting. I'd had no idea that one of my strongest potential allies in the fight for the inclusion of pregnant girls in schools occupied an office one floor below mine. I hadn't even known her position on the issue.

I was not sure what shocked me more—the scale and depth of Madam Gogra's service, or the fact that I was only learning about it now. Upon further reflection, I wondered if she hadn't been trying to tell me this all along, but I had not listened closely enough to hear her.

Madam Gogra attributed the success of the program to her ability to listen to both the students and their parents. "We need the whole package, Minister," she concluded, right before the program was called to order. As it turned out, Madam Gogra had already provided one possible answer to Gloria's question, which was how the state would support the pregnant girls and their families. We just needed to scale up some of what she had been doing.

Over the next months, as I continued my travels around the country, I met countless young mothers who, against all odds, were finding their ways back to school. I talked to boys, too, and soon learned that the fight for inclusion was equally important for them.

In Moyamba District, in the south of Sierra Leone, a boy I'll call Joe approached me after a town hall and introduced himself to me as a male parent learner. Joe was neither tall nor large, but he had a muscular frame and a deep voice—he could have passed for a rugby player. Though he had just turned eighteen,

Joe had a son who was almost one year old. When I enquired about the boy's mother, he said his sixteen-year-old girlfriend had dropped out of school to take care of their son. He loved his girlfriend and they'd had sex only once, he confided.

I could tell there was something he wanted to get off his chest, so I steered him away from the crowd and toward a mango tree, where we could get some shade and privacy. As we sat on a flat rock, he began to cry. I told him it was OK to be emotional, but he quickly pulled himself together. A cool breeze dried his face, wafting away the musky scent of his sweat.

When he was able to resume, he told me that the one time they'd had sex was after a school prize ceremony at which she'd collected several awards. They'd considered abortion but there was no safe and legal option available to them. "We chose life," he said. My eyes watered up a bit and I looked away. "No judgment," I told him. I added that I would not have known what to do myself if I had been faced with a similar challenge.

Listening without judgment is something I'd learned from professor and author Brené Brown's book *Dare to Lead*. She provides several tools for leaders to promote empathy, encouraging them to "rumble" with vulnerability: that is, to be willing to listen and interact, trusting others enough to share potentially divisive ideas with them. The more power you have over others, the more empathy and patience you need to show in order to encourage them to share their full and authentic views. This applies not just to government ministers but to managers in companies and to parents, to name just two of the many types of people who hold sway over others. We all need to remember that it takes a lot of strength to speak truth to power, to voice something that is in opposition to the views of someone who can affect your life and destiny, so it's important that those in positions of authority give people all the time and the space that they need to express themselves, however they choose.

I assured Joe that I heard him, and that I understood the shame, regret, and, most important, the guilt he was feeling. If he could, he told me, he would have given up his own place in school for his girlfriend, who he believed was smarter than him. "What is going to happen with her now?" he asked, as his tears began to flow again.

Many people in favor of the ban like to argue that the boys who are responsible for the pregnancies should also be banned from school if they are students. There's an undeniable logic to the idea, but it would be totally counterproductive. Also denying young fathers an education would only compound the problem. After hearing this many times, I came to believe that people cling to it as a dodge, lest they be forced to admit that denying anyone an education is fundamentally unjust.

Joe put a face and a name to a group of people everyone, including myself, had completely ignored. Listening to him, I realized that radical inclusion applies to male parent learners no less than pregnant girls. Joe told me he was more determined than ever to do well at school, complete his education, and get a job so he could take care of his family. The answer can never be to compound an injustice, only to remove it. Instead of banning people like Joe from schools, we need to support them.

Active listening—listening to understand and to learn—is a critical skill for leaders and for anyone else who seeks to advocate for justice and change social norms.

It was a skill I'd honed as a member of the biomechatronics group at the MIT Media Lab, working under my adviser and mentor, Professor Hugh Herr. The lab champions human-centered design in the development of various kinds of prostheses and other medical devices. "Human-centered" means that we interviewed patients about their needs and desires right at the start, and that we kept them in the loop at every stage as key members of the team.

My own research was on prosthetic sockets, which I believed could be improved by bringing together the capabilities of magnetic resonance imaging, soft tissue modeling, and 3-D printing. Some of my colleagues in the lab advised against using the techniques I had proposed because they were so novel—which was exactly why I was so determined to succeed. I'm just stubborn, I guess; I wanted to accomplish the impossible.

Sockets are notoriously difficult to design because they have to be custom fit to each patient—and also be light and comfortable. Because they are the point of connection between the human body and the prosthetic, they are its most important part. Professor Herr—a double below-knee amputee himself—didn't just advise me, he also volunteered to test all the iterations of my socket. Over a period of five years, he tried on many designs that broke during testing.

As difficult as we knew it would be to achieve our objective, we remained laser-focused on our hypotheses and the mathematics. The human body is made of multi-material components—skin, muscles, blood vessels, bones, etc.—with variable impedances; any load-bearing interface interacting with it must also be multi-material to prevent soft tissue damage and pressure sores, we argued. While the research was intellectually stimulating, it was also very personal for both of us. I believed that veterans and victims of Sierra Leone's civil war who had suffered amputations would be better integrated and included in society if they had comfortable prostheses that worked for them.

One day Hugh and I were evaluating a new 3-D–printed design at the lab. We were unsure whether it would fit because

I had made an error in the calculation and shrunk the design by about five millimeters. We were also not sure whether it would be load bearing or break during testing because of a design choice I made. Hugh was too excited to wait for further calculations; he wanted to walk in the "sexy" sockets that felt like he was "walking on pillows." First, he walked within a guided walkway with bars on either side, and then he wanted to walk freely from one end of the room to the other. I asked him if he was sure he was OK and he said yes. But when he was only halfway across the room, one of the sockets cracked and he began to collapse. I barely caught him in time.

After that, I realized I needed to pay as much attention to what people *didn't* say as to what they did say. People will answer the same question differently based on who asks it and whether they are or aren't in the mood to please the questioner. Part of active listening is paying attention to people's facial expressions and body language. You have to make sure you understand your own motivation behind asking the questions you do, too—and why someone might answer with total candor or be more reluctant to do so.

When I talked about pregnant girls in schools, I heard lots of objections based on fixed ideas about morality. I'd hoped to avoid religious arguments, but you can't change people's minds unless you fully understand the nature of their objections and learn where you might have room to combat them.

The education ministry is a co-organizer of an annual Education Week, during which stakeholders come together to discuss current issues and develop a vision for the future of education in Sierra Leone. At the first of these following the president's reaffirmation of the ban, the ministry's chief education officer outlined our plans to develop and roll out a program called the National Policy on Radical Inclusion in Schools, which would allow visibly pregnant girls to attend classes in person. When she finished her presentation, she invited stakeholders to share their questions or offer suggestions on implementation. At first, no one even mentioned the ban. I hoped this was because everyone was aligned with our views by now; we had engaged the media extensively, and I had been traveling the country for weeks to discuss the issue in person.

But I was dead wrong.

As soon as there was a lull in the questions, an older man in the back—he looked to be in his seventies—rose to his feet. Identifying himself as a religious leader, he said he wanted to "warn the minister and his team" about this new policy, because he and his peers would not accept it. "What should we tell our congregations?" he bellowed. It was a question, but it wasn't. I was seated in the front row and, after looking behind me to see him, I turned back around and looked straight ahead. He went on to rail that it was policies like this one that were responsible for the poor quality of education and the high immorality we had in our country. These "Western policies" were not for us, he concluded.

"I am sure the minister will respond to your concerns," the chief education officer said, motioning for me to join her on stage. I could well understand why she wanted to pass the ball. I got up from my chair and took the microphone.

"Thank you very much for your concern, sir. I am grateful that you are comfortable to share your beliefs at a forum like this," I began. "This was precisely the goal of this dialogue, to imagine and shape the future of education for our children." I meant what I said. Sure, I would have loved it if everyone was on board with the program, but if they weren't I wanted to hear about it so we could explore their objections together.

I first asked if there was anything else that he wanted to say about the issue. "No," he replied. Then I proceeded to ask him a couple of rhetorical questions:

"Do pregnant schoolgirls currently go to mosque or church and sit alongside non-pregnant girls, or do we send them to a different religious house? If they do attend together, have pregnant girls sitting next to non-pregnant girls led to the latter becoming pregnant? In religious houses, we preach that sinners should come to the house of God for healing, teaching, and forgiveness. Have pregnant girls fallen so far that we should tell them to give up all hope? Do we advise God-fearing and tradition-minding parents to build different bedrooms, different marketplaces, and different playgrounds for pregnant girls?"

Sierra Leone is a very religious country; I could see that my questions hit a nerve. "I am religious myself," I continued, in the hope of easing some of the tension. "Though I am a practicing Catholic, most of my extended family is Muslim. One of my grandfathers with whom I spent a lot of time during my childhood was an imam in the neighborhood mosque and I observed Ramadan with him."

You may wonder what this has to do with active listening since it was I who was doing all the talking. But the reason I was able to pursue this line of logic was because I had in fact engaged in extended periods of active listening with just about every religious figure I knew.

I told the questioner that I had engaged the head of my church on this topic and discussed it at length with various priests in the different churches that I attended in Freetown and Bo. Hardly any of them questioned the decision to overturn the ban. I had also engaged my Muslim uncles in the village. They felt as the priests did—that it wasn't a problem that could or should be adjudicated by religion. Being pregnant isn't a sin, they said. The violation of the girl's body that led to the pregnancy is the sin, and a particularly egregious one if the person doing so is older or it is against the girl's wishes. This was the view of all of their religions and of every religion in Sierra Leone.

I paused and then said that I would try to answer the specific question he had asked, which was what religious leaders should tell their congregations. I suggested they tell them that we were failing to protect our children.

The church or mosque and the state are different institutions, I pointed out. Both have vested interests in morality and justice, but it is the state that makes the national laws. I reminded him that adding religious polarization to policy-making is a recipe for disaster in an already politically and ethnically divided state like Sierra Leone. By the time I ended my response, the religious leader seemed to be smiling—though it was impossible to tell if he was convinced or just humoring me to bring the conversation to an end. Finally, I heard him say, "OK." My colleagues sighed with relief.

I subsequently raised the topic in churches and mosques all over Sierra Leone. In one church I attended in the east end of Freetown, the priest himself spoke explicitly about radical inclusion and the role that parents and community members needed to play to protect our girls. The problem, he said, was rape culture; what we really need to concentrate on as a nation is reducing the number of girls who become pregnant, not stopping the ones who do from attending classes.

Active listening helped me counter the arguments of religious leaders who supported the ban, but it also showed me that my fear that religious leaders would vehemently and universally oppose overturning it was a myth. Many of my key talking points came from priests and imams.

Here's the thing about listening: the more I listened, the more I realized how much I didn't know and how essential it was to engage with all kinds of people, from all walks of life, and from every part of the country.

So, my colleagues and I packed our bags and set out to engage citizens where they lived—in their communities in cities but also in those remote areas labeled as "hard to reach." We held public engagements and had deeper conversations with small groups of local leaders and subgroups like women's and youth groups. We sat with children, parents, teachers, chiefs, civil society organizations, local council leaders, journalists, and anyone else who wanted to listen or tell us about the challenges they faced and explain to us their ways of solving the kinds of problems that forever plague the education sector. We prayed, laughed, cried, argued, and danced together; there were road accidents that destroyed some of the team members' vehicles but thankfully didn't result in any major injuries. The rules of engagement were simple—honest discussion powered by empathy and respect.

At each stop, the makeup of the participants was different.

Wherever we could, we invited pregnant girls to speak. But before they did, I set some important limits on the kind of listening I was willing to engage in.

The problem was that some local leaders, often male, would take the microphone and blame the girls for their pregnancies. "These girls are not serious," they would say. "They are chasing men for mobile phones and money." At first, I would not respond, but I quickly learned to intervene when such views were expressed because I didn't want the girls who had bravely shown up at the meetings to be further harmed psychologically, knowing how many of them were victims of gender-based violence.

"Excuse me, sir," I would interrupt. "If a woman—I mean, a child, comes to you and takes off her panties and begs you to have sex with her for free, wouldn't you refuse and do everything in your power to let her parents and care providers know and get her the help she needs?" Often, the leaders were shocked to hear those words come out of the mouth of an adult male, never mind a senior government official, but it was important that I responded when I heard sentiments of victim-blaming.

I learned that I needed to be mindful of the difference between listening to all perspectives and tolerating abuse that further marginalized the most vulnerable in our communities. You can't let comments stand that are clearly intended to normalize or trivialize inequalities. That sometimes means treading a fine line, because I don't want to alienate potential allies.

Still, I trust that it is possible to disagree with people firmly and even vociferously without necessarily making an enemy of them for life. I learned this very early, because that's how I was raised. My father and I argued, or rather debated, every topic imaginable, sometimes unpleasantly—but we always ended on a note of respect, if not exactly acceptance of each other's positions. Often, we would just change the subject.

As a young cabinet minister in a country like Sierra Leone, where younger people do not typically disagree with elders, particularly in public, I had to work harder to stay calm. During one of my first community meetings, I voiced my disagreement with an idea presented by an older participant; I thought my objection was innocuous. That evening, my mother, who was not present at the meeting, rang me feeling very worried because the community leader whose views I had failed to endorse had called her to say that I had been disrespectful. She laughed as she reminded me of a story from my childhood.

My Uncle F. O., now a canon in the Anglican church, loved to tell stories. When he did, he did not like to be interrupted with questions, especially if they came from me. It is family legend that whenever Uncle F. O. was telling a story and I arrived on the scene, everyone tensed up, knowing that

I would inevitably interrupt with a question and that Uncle F. O. would refuse to continue until I left. My siblings and cousins would stare me down, silently pleading with me to hold my tongue. Sometimes I could, but often I couldn't. I just needed to understand why or how something happened.

At UWC in Norway and at college in the United States, I had gotten into the habit of asking even more questions. When I finished my master's thesis, Kate bought me a bust of Socrates as a gift in line with the nickname my friends gave me: the Question Master of the Royal Society of Question Masters, a made-up organization we all belonged to because of our love of asking questions. This bust sits on my desk at the office.

I had learned from my mentors that we must always ask questions. What attracted me to the leadership style of President Obama was his love of asking questions and weighing all kinds of views when faced with critical decisions. President Obama loved asking questions so much that during a televised speech to schoolchildren in 2009, he said, "Don't be afraid to ask questions. Don't be afraid to ask for help when you need it. I do that every day. Asking for help isn't a sign of weakness, it's a sign of strength. It shows you have the courage to admit when you don't know something, and to learn something new."

I remember watching snippets of that talk back then and

feeling a bit sad that I had been reprimanded as a child for doing what he said. In other writings and speeches, President Obama made a point of emphasizing how much he consults with different experts, opinion makers, and opposition stakeholders. In his book *A Promised Land,* he shares how he persuaded Michelle Obama that he should run for president. He said, "The day I raise my right hand and take the oath to be the president of the United States, the world will start looking at America differently. I know that kids all around this country—Black kids, Hispanic kids, kids who don't fit in—they'll see themselves differently, too."

Whether it was Einstein hunkering down to understand a problem deeply by himself, or Dr. Robert Livingston having thousands of hours of uncomfortable conversations, it's hard work to get to the essence of a problem. Once that is done, the question then becomes what your role is in solving the problem. For Barack Obama, the way to address the systemic exclusion of "kids who don't fit in" was to run for and win the presidency. For me and my team in Sierra Leone, the question was how we could play our roles in such a way that we inspired others to get involved.

3

Define Your Role—
Why You, Why Now?

· · · · ·

Each one of us has an essential role in the whole of humanity.

—OPRAH WINFREY

The most common question grown-ups ask schoolchildren after "What's your name?" and "How old are you?" is "What do you want to be when you grow up?" Children learn to say their name as one of their first words and obsessively track their ages and upcoming birthdays as soon as they learn the numbers two or three. But many people still don't know what they want to become when they grow up, even when they're young adults. And that's OK. Oprah Winfrey, Ralph Lauren, and many others were on seemingly different paths in their twenties compared to where they are today.

Even as a kid I never enjoyed answering that question because it presupposed that I could become only one thing. And worse, once you decided what that one thing was, your family and your friends would hold you to it and you were meant to devote your entire life to making it happen. I wanted to become so many things, how was I to choose only one? But when I did care to respond, like most children I had a ready-made answer: "I would like to be a medical doctor like Dr. J. C. Boima." The adults questioning me then thought they had their answer. "Oh, you want to be a doctor, how wonderful!" But that wasn't what I was saying at all. I didn't just want to be a doctor—I wanted to be a doctor like my uncle, Dr. J. C. Boima.

To the world, Dr. Boima, or J. C., as he was called by his contemporaries, was a renowned specialist surgeon. To me, he was so much more. He was my hero. Nothing made me happier as a child than when my uncle let me shadow him in the operating theater, which I began doing for hours at a time before I'd even turned ten. I watched him save lives and while he was at it, he taught me anatomy. But that's not the main reason I wanted to be like him—I wanted to serve people the way he did and make a difference in the world.

My uncle would operate on people whether they could afford the fees or not—and he would buy medicines for them and pay their transportation to and from their homes when they couldn't themselves. For several years he was a cabinet minister, but he still taught at the university, did clinical rounds at the government hospitals, and saw patients every week at his clinics in Freetown and Bo. Dr. Boima was trained in Germany and had numerous offers to stay but felt called to return to Sierra Leone. When he became desperately ill and almost died during our civil war, he was evacuated to Germany. After he recovered, he was offered a lucrative job there, but he packed his bags and returned home again to serve his people.

I was quite good at mathematics and the sciences in school. My dad, a former teacher, helped me with my homework, and I had access to mathematics books my grandfather had authored. Even as a small child, I recognized my good fortune in being a member of an educated family. I knew that attending school was the utmost privilege and something that should not be denied to any child. By the time I was in high school, I had chosen to study the sciences and was well on the path to being a medical doctor.

But the more I thought about my uncle's record of service, the more I realized that I could serve even more people if I was a medical doctor, a biomedical engineer, and a researcher all in one. I made up my mind to pursue a joint MD/PhD degree.

At home, I always volunteered to set up every gadget my parents bought. There were times I had excess screws in my hand after turning on a device and I would have to take it apart again while I figured out what I had done wrong, much to the frustration of my many cousins, who were eager to see the device in action. In college, I took premed courses, sat for the MCAT, and fulfilled all the other requirements to enroll in medical school—but then chose not to do so. I figured that it would be easier to incorporate medicine into my desire to build devices that would help people than to do the opposite. As it happened, my PhD research in biomedical sciences and prosthetic design did bring me close to patients. For a while, I was satisfied with medical engineering and research, but I should have known that I would not only find myself wanting to be involved in public service, but that I would be drawn to the field of education. It was written in my genes. Some might say it was my destiny.

It is well known that my grandmother, Mama Bee, would leave a bucket of cool water under a tree outside her home in Gobaru for schoolchildren to drink on their way to and from school. My maternal grandfather, David Solomon Moinina Lahai (whose names I carry), widely known as DSM or Teacher Lahai, was a lifelong educator. At home, we called him Maada. The first person in his village to go to school, Maada pursued his higher studies in Sierra Leone, Kenya, and the United Kingdom. Eventually he rose to the position of math coordinator within the Ministry of Education, where he served for close to fifty years. My mother, Ngo Lizzy, took after her dad. She joined the civil service and worked as a secretary and a clerk in the Pujehun District education office for ten years, until political violence intervened in 1982, when she and her entire family were beaten and chased out of Pujehun Town by thugs of the government for supporting her uncle's campaign for Parliament as a member of the Sierra Leone People's Party. After my parents and older siblings moved to Bo, where I was born, my mom served for another twenty-nine years in the district education office, retiring in 2012. Nearly all of Ngo Lizzy's siblings are either currently serving or formerly served as teachers, head teachers, or principals.

My father, Paul, is a lifelong educator as well. He taught physics and mathematics in secondary school immediately after completing his own secondary education. After university, he returned to the classroom for several years before he began his long career in the development sector, working at the Ministry of Health and Sanitation, the Ministry of Gender, Children and Women's Affairs, and for UNICEF Sierra Leone. Several of my own siblings obtained teacher qualification degrees and taught in the classroom or became administrators or civil servants in the department of education.

So, it's no coincidence that I ended up in education. After I achieved my childhood dream of combining medicine, engineering, and research, and of working directly with people who needed care, I, too, like Maada, Mama Bee, and Ngo Lizzy before me, came to believe that it was not enough just to support public education—so I made it my life's goal to ensure that everyone has access to it.

The fight over the ban on pregnant girls was thrust upon me by events that were out of my control. But it caused me to ponder the general dilemma of how we figure out what we need to do in the world—where to lend our talents—and what problems we should try to solve.

There are many seemingly intractable challenges in our lives, our communities, and society, many of which have persisted for generations. Institutional racism; hatred of people with different sexual orientations; the exclusion of people with disabilities; maternal mortality and other global health challenges; the impacts of economic inequality; climate change; and gender-based violence, to name just a few.

While all these challenges are significant, aspects of many of them are being addressed. For that reason, various intellectuals including cognitive psychologist and professor Steven Pinker and professor of international health Hans Rosling proposed that the world is indeed getting better when you look at global metrics. That is good news for both realists and optimists, and there is a lot of evidence and research to support it. Professor Rosling, I should add, didn't consider himself an optimist but rather a "possibilist," pointing out that the evidence suggested it is possible to make positive change—*if* we have the facts we need and the will to do so. There are now several countries where same-sex marriage is legal, the global homicide rate is declining, fewer children and mothers are dying from preventable diseases, and there are many more girls in school today than there ever were before.

Yet for some of those challenges, progress has been elusive. Climate change is worsening; racial tensions persist; sexual and gender-based violence remains a big problem globally; and economic inequality is widening. And when we disaggregate the data and look into specific communities, even the positive results turn out to tell a different story. In many instances, women and girls living in remote areas are worse off than they have been for a very long time.

Advances in science and technology and stronger multilateral global institutions continue to have an immense positive impact, but the actions and sacrifices of activists, innovators, disruptors, social entrepreneurs, individual citizens, and community organizations are still key. While it is true that sometimes the odds are stacked against individuals who are trying to make change, it is certain that without them change won't happen swiftly, if ever.

I find it inspiring and instructive to ask the changemakers I most admire what made them ask those two all-important questions of themselves: "Why me?" and "Why now?" Their answers are almost never simple; there's usually a long story for each of them.

Marshall Ganz, a social organizer from Harvard Kennedy School, developed a well-known social change theory called "public narrative" which is rooted in three things: the story of self, the story of us, and the story of now. For there to be a solution to any social challenge, the individuals working for change must understand and effectively communicate through stories what motivated them to take action. This is the story of self. Ganz suggests that it's through sharing the choices and decisions we make as individuals that we inspire others to get involved.

Then, we need to build a shared vision: the story of us. That's a variation on "Why me?" How will the singular "you" inspire and become the plural "you"?

Finally, the story of now speaks to taking action with urgency. Why can't this issue wait? What makes it urgent? There has to be a story for that, too.

American author Mark Twain is quoted as saying: "The two most important days of your life are the day you are born and the day you find out why." Growing up, I saw Dr. Boima as a model for selfless public service and for doing everything you can to help others. I ultimately found comfort in pursuing work in the field of education for all. But just knowing that I wanted to pursue a life of public service in education wasn't enough to provide the kinds of practical answers I needed. Whenever possible, I try to meet changemakers of every kind. It is from their examples that I find the wisdom and inspiration that I need.

I engage in conversations about passion and purpose with mentors, friends, and colleagues everywhere, but I especially enjoy the chance to talk over a meal. There's something about breaking bread together. In Boston and Nairobi and now in Freetown, Kate and I regularly host people from different backgrounds—including schoolchildren, award-winning artists, young entrepreneurs, political leaders, activists, and world-renowned experts—over home-cooked meals to laugh and share knowledge.

One such dinner guest in Freetown was the late Dr. Paul Farmer, a world leader in global health and medicine who is best known for his transformational role in institutional capacity building in Rwanda and the fight against drug-resistant tuberculosis in Haiti. Paul had been a mentor, professor, and friend to me since my days as an undergraduate at Harvard. Over a spicy home-cooked meal one night, he addressed the questions "Why you?" and "Why now?"

From rural villages in Haiti and Rwanda, to prisons in Siberia, to inner-city neighborhoods in Boston, Paul and the organizations he worked with had a simple goal: alleviate poverty and reduce inequity by providing quality healthcare and other services for the world's poorest. While he considered himself an optimist, Paul was very aware of the challenges he faced. This was why he wanted his work to be fully integrated in the communities he served. He believed that the answer to "Why you?" for an individual must be driven by a collective "Why you?" for the community being served. Underpinning his work was the inclusion of his former patients and local staff who were trained to do the same work the foreign experts began.

As for the question "Why now?" he believed the answer depended on the context of each community. It is difficult to achieve positive clinical outcomes when the issues affecting the patients are related to poverty and hunger. To heal a patient, you might have to provide them with food and shelter, too.

Following these examples, I realized that sometimes we need to ask ourselves not just "Why me?" but also "Who other than me?" When we are addressing problems, it's crucial to consider the possibility that we might not be the right person to address a particular problem at a particular time; maybe because the problem isn't the one that most urgently needs solving, or maybe because someone else is far better suited to the challenge than we are—and our own involvement may be robbing them of the opportunity to act. This is a subtle point and shouldn't be used as an excuse for inaction. But I saw in Paul's work that his long-term successes were driven by the knowledge that he needed to exit as soon as the local stakeholders he worked with had learned what they needed to complete the job at hand, which they could usually do much better than he and his team.

Paul came to this knowledge by listening with empathy to the needs of the community, in particular the poor and his local colleagues. In 2022, at age sixty-two, he died in his sleep during a clinical mission in northern Rwanda. I miss him more than I can say, but his example continues to inspire me.

Another person who's taught me a great deal about how to answer the questions "Why you?" and "Why now?" is my countrymate Dr. Humarr Kahn, who coincidentally was a colleague of Paul's. Unfortunately, I didn't know him personally. Dr. Kahn died of Ebola at age thirty-nine during the 2014 epidemic. But I got the chance to hear inspiring stories about his life and sacrifice from a fellow cabinet minister who was one of his close friends and colleagues.

Dr. Austin Demby is currently Sierra Leone's minister of health and sanitation, but he was a director at the US Department of Health and Human Services on Friday, July 18, 2014, when Dr. Kahn made the clinical rounds at a hot, crowded, and poorly ventilated Ebola ward in Kenema Government Hospital. At a dinner at my home, he recalled watching him from a distance as he provided care to the patients. One of the patients he comforted was a nurse Dr. Demby had recruited himself several decades earlier.

The following Monday, Dr. Kahn reported his first symptoms. Over the next seven days, the discussions about his care reached the highest levels of government, both in Sierra Leone and around the world. But any chance of evacuation to a more advanced medical system ended with his untimely death, a disaster that underlined the health and economic disparities we face in our country. The global response to the epidemic was woefully uncoordinated. Even after the reality of the situation could be clearly seen, too little was done too slowly, causing the needless loss of thousands of lives in West Africa.

Sadly, it's a lesson we fail to learn again and again. If we had listened to the health practitioners who were on the front lines during the Ebola outbreak, we could have been better prepared for the COVID-19 pandemic, which has killed millions of people. Why don't we learn from our mistakes? Why don't more global health officials ask the right questions of themselves and of others so they can find the right role to play?

Dr. Kahn knew his role: he was there to serve and provide healthcare—the best care—to his patients, even after he joined them in their ward. He remained hopeful to the end, inspiring his colleagues to give their all.

Here's what inspires me the most: when the Ebola outbreak began, Dr. Kahn was overseeing the Lassa fever ward. Lassa is also a hemorrhagic virus, albeit one that is far less contagious and deadly than Ebola. But there were risks; Lassa had killed his immediate predecessor. Even so, when Ebola emerged, Dr. Kahn didn't hesitate to lead the effort to contain it, and not just as a researcher and community leader, but as a clinician. At the time of his death, he had directly treated and saved the lives of over one hundred Ebola patients. He loved his patients, loved his community, loved his country, and—as the person leading Sierra Leone's only specialized treatment ward for hemorrhagic fever and, as such, the face of the nation's response to the disease—he accepted his role with grace, dedication, and service.

But simply answering "Why you?" and "Why now?" is not enough. To have the kind of impact that is needed to make inroads on intractable problems, we need to understand the role *all people* play, those who consciously choose to get involved and those who stand by passively, those who advance the debate deliberately and those who hold it back, perhaps without even knowing it.

Often individuals, especially those who aren't actively

involved, are not explicitly aware of the roles they play or how they reinforce the status quo by standing on the sidelines. One effective technique to change that is to take them through a kind of audit: to work with them to help them see what their actions and positions mean in practice.

This technique is particularly important when it comes to the press and media. Humans are social beings, so what we think others believe shapes our positions on issues, even if subconsciously. This is especially true when the others in question come from a similar background, or we share other affiliations. People want to be part of a group. The media plays a powerful role in enforcing the status quo, but it can also spur on movements for social change. It's truly a double-edged sword.

When it came to the ban on pregnant girls in schools, I believed, like Paul Farmer, that our life's work must be in sync with the community. Emulating Dr. Kahn, who rose to his role when the occasion demanded it, as minister of basic and senior secondary education I accepted the challenge to fight for universal access to education.

I knew the story of me, but I had to broaden it by helping to create the story of us that was not just for my team, but for the larger society. I decided to do this by being more of a mirror than a cudgel—by playing back to people what I heard and what I saw. If I could get people to see the issues in a different light, some, at least, would join us. To do this at scale, I needed to convince the media.

For the most part, the popular media had projected the same myths and perceptions that supported the ban. But having understood my role, I was now ready to engage. I picked up my phone and called Asmaa James at Radio Democracy. *Good Morning Salone* is the most widely listened to radio talk show in Sierra Leone. Broadcast on weekdays from 7:30 A.M. to 9 A.M. on Radio Democracy 98.1 FM, its regular audience runs the gamut of senior citizens, students, traders, and senior government officials. The show is perceived by the public as tough; Asmaa James and her mostly female co-hosts have been known to bring heads of government agencies to their knees. They ask challenging questions and include unfiltered comments from the public; many guests complain they were ambushed. While I am generally confident in interviews, I get nervous whenever I am on *Good Morning Salone*; knowing that the president and vice president often tune in only compounds my dread.

When Asmaa agreed to have me on, I was well aware of both the risks and the opportunities it presented. Asmaa and the other hosts were all in favor of the ban, so while on the one hand it was the biggest platform I could ever ask for from which to debate my position, I could set my cause back irrecoverably if I didn't do well.

After the initial pleasantries, Asmaa went straight for the jugular: "Mr. Minister, wouldn't allowing pregnant girls in school undermine the government's flagship Free Quality School Education program? Does it also not contradict the first lady's Hands Off Our Girls campaign?" As I thought about the question and how to begin my response, I noticed the sound of the air conditioner in the room. Its thermostat was set to sixty-six degrees Fahrenheit, but I wondered if it was working because I suddenly felt sweat running down my ribs.

This question was especially tough because one of President Bio's most important goals is the success of the Free Quality School Education program. Making a connection between the ban on pregnant girls and the president's legacy was meant to drive a wedge between me and the president. Gathering my strength, I dropped my shoulders and leaned in toward the microphone.

Asmaa beckoned me to relax by raising her hands up and down slowly. This was not the first time she had done this while I was in her studio. During my earlier appearances on the show, she had observed that I was easily unsettled by questions I thought I had addressed already or that I considered unfair. I knew I could not sound dismissive, agitated, or be impolite. I also knew that Asmaa was doing me a great favor by asking me a tough and direct question: she was giving me the opportunity to tackle it head-on. It is what good journalists do. I took a deep breath, smiled at Asmaa, and remembered that I had gone there to help others understand my position. She was their proxy; I had to win her over.

"Yes, there's a clear link between the policy to allow pregnant girls back to school and the president's vision," I said slowly. One of the hosts was surprised; perhaps she'd expected me to be defensive. "The idea to have accessible, tuition-free, quality education is intricately linked to having every child go to school—your child, my child, and the child of the market woman. And this includes children with disabilities, poor children, and victims of sexual abuse. Pregnant schoolgirls are generally victims of sexual abuse." The president's aggressive agenda to address rape culture and sexual violence and the first lady's Hands Off Our Girls campaign were all about inclusion, I added.

The first lady must have been listening to the show because she sent me a text message right after it was over, while I was still in the studio, saying she would like to be involved in further conversations on the topic. She didn't sound fully convinced, which was good to know, if only because she was definitely someone who could be a powerful ally. It was important for me to find a way to get her to become a partner in the story of us, whether or not she had a story of me. I decided I needed to pivot my arguments more toward national inclusion. I needed to make it about what excluding a group of people says about us as a nation, and how it doesn't align with our values.

Once known as the "Athens of West Africa" for its level of education, Sierra Leone was one of the first countries in our region to establish publicly accessible boys' and girls' secondary schools. Sierra Leone also set up the first Western-style university in sub-Saharan Africa in 1827. Men and women from all tribes, religions, and countries came to Freetown for an education.

I felt like I was making progress. After an intense ninety-minute discussion, I detected a slight hesitation in Asmaa's responses. At one point, she dragged her chair in toward the table; in that moment, I felt her position on the topic shift as well. After the interview, I read through the comments section on the program's social media feed and the SMS text messages sent in by listeners.

While many listeners' positions had not changed, large numbers of messages were from people advocating for more inclusion. As the show continued, the tenor of the comments shifted from blaming the pregnant girls to asking the government to ensure they would be protected if they returned to school. People were starting to focus on the lack of consequences faced by perpetrators. Most important of all, the issue was clearly on the table. People were willing to entertain arguments against the ban, even if they were not fully convinced.

I had been on many shows as a public official and had talked about some challenging issues, but this program felt different. I could see a pivot happening in real time: more citizens were now supporting our vision, and some of them had been among our fiercest opponents. We'd moved them by challenging them to choose a side: one of universal access and inclusion or one of veiled exclusion hiding behind a dubious appeal to morality. There's a saying: "If someone's liberation upsets you, there is a good chance you were benefiting from their oppression."

Before I left the station, Asmaa called me into her office and asked me for data on the number of pregnant girls who would be affected should the cabinet overturn the ban. I told her I would get back to her and left in a buoyant mood. My office is less than two minutes away from the Radio Democracy station. As my car pulled up in front of the building, my phone buzzed. I checked my messages, and it was a thumbs-up emoji from the president, who had also been listening. He's a man of few words, but his emoji was all I needed. If Asmaa and President Bio were now among the "us" group, then we were off to a great start.

I got several calls from other media houses inviting me to engage on the topic. The next day, I appeared on the Sierra

Leone Broadcasting Corporation's (SLBC) morning radio show. I then appeared on the two major television talk shows on SLBC and the African Young Voices TV. The hosts of both shows started out by arguing for the ban. They didn't say that's what they themselves believed, but they presented it as the opinion of the nation. But by the end of both shows, I could see that the hosts and their audiences had softened their views a little bit.

My original intention had been to get the general public on our side, but I quickly learned that the ones paying closest attention and whose positions were changing most rapidly were my colleagues in government, and in particular, at the Ministry of Education. They, too, were hearing positive comments and messages from their own circles as the debate shifted. In one of the first meetings I led as a minister, several members of my senior staff either turned away, laughed, or audibly murmured "no" when I told them my position on the ban. Those same colleagues were now with "us," and the burden felt a bit lighter.

As before, I learned to use my own family as something of a bellwether or at least a sounding board. One day Kadija came back from school while the younger girls and I were sitting in the living room, singing along to Coldplay's "Green Eyes" as I casually strummed the guitar. After a while, she asked whether the government would tell the parents of pregnant girls about their reproductive status if the girls didn't want them to know. I was a bit surprised at the question, but I put my guitar down to pay closer attention. That was when I realized that she and her classmates, too, were discussing the topic. They say that fresh air and sunlight are the best disinfectants. Clearly, they were starting to make a difference. Kadija's views were evolving.

On my subsequent travels across Sierra Leone, I received invitations to many local radio stations. I accepted all of them and was happy to answer whatever they asked me. When a journalist did not bring up the ban directly, I would find a way to introduce it into the conversation. I wanted the public to keep engaging with the topic so I could bring the myths around it to light and remove any taboos.

The constant debating took me right back to my secondary school days, when I participated in debate competitions. This time, however, I had been practicing my lines over an extended period of time, to all kinds of audiences. There were no judges and no medals to keep me going—just the hope that thousands of girls would have a chance at a better life if we succeeded.

Don't get me wrong. I still knew that the majority of the nation, including most of those in government who were now encouraging me, were not yet sold on the idea that it was time to overturn the ban. I also knew that I couldn't read too much

into the president's thumbs-up. Just because he was in favor
of my bringing this discussion to the people didn't at all mean
that he was ready to go back on the policy he had endorsed
with such conviction. Getting people on board to do something sometime is one thing. Getting them to agree that we
need to do something right now is quite another.

Once it is clear why you (singular and plural "you") must
be part of a change or movement, the timing is the next major
factor. Why is now the best time? What about the current so-
ciopolitical climate makes it possible for change to take place
successfully? If pursued at the wrong time or in the wrong
space, outcomes can be very different. That doesn't argue for
not pursuing social change whenever you see inequity; it just
means you need to be cognizant of the forces arrayed against
you, and be in it for the long haul. This is just one of the many
lessons I learned from the Civil Rights Movement in America.

Although Rosa Parks is a crucial and important figure
in the history of Black resistance to segregation, she was not
the first Black woman to refuse orders from a bus driver in
Montgomery, Alabama. Nine months earlier, fifteen-year-old
Claudette Colvin had also refused to give up her seat on a bus
and was arrested and sent to jail. Her case was reported in
the local media, but it didn't make international news, spark
a Supreme Court case, elevate Dr. Martin Luther King, Jr.'s

activist platform, or start the bus boycott that would ultimately lead to major social change. There are many reasons for this, but Colvin, who ultimately was one of the four plaintiffs to give testimony to the Supreme Court that resulted in the ruling that ended segregation on municipal buses, has said that it was because she didn't have the right story to mobilize the movement. More likely it was because of her timing.

Colvin became pregnant soon after her arrest and she believed that made the National Association for the Advancement of Colored People (NAACP) reluctant to use her as a public symbol. As we know, the idea of teenage pregnancy being a moral shame is nothing new. But Colvin's protest played a crucial role in building up the momentum for Parks and the boycott that followed. While change may seem to erupt all of a sudden, it is most often the result of generations of actions.

The length of time it takes to make change can vary enormously. The North African Arab Spring lasted a very short time and yet national leaders and regimes were toppled in several countries, whereas Nelson Mandela was imprisoned for twenty-seven years before apartheid collapsed in South Africa. How do we know when now is the time to act, and if it is not, what do we do? The truth is we can't know before trying, but the timing of actions that can lead to system-level change largely depends on whether a much-needed coalition of citizen stakeholders believes the time for change could not be any better than it is now.

My friend Chernor Bah runs a feminist organization in Sierra Leone called Purposeful. A committed activist, he has fought for girls' education for most of his life. In fact, he wrote several articles on the need to overturn the ban on pregnant girls after the previous government announced it. As part of his advocacy, he held several meetings with senior government officials, including the former president of Sierra Leone. But while he had clearly identified the problem and got to work addressing it, the ban still remained. I learned a lot from his experience, noting in particular the need for a broader coalition to advocate for the change and the timing of the action.

About a year before Dr. Boima's passing (I can't express how much I miss him), I met him for a drink. He was on his way home from the hospital and I'd had a long day, so we chose a location close to my office. He asked for just water and I ordered a malt soft drink. As we spoke about any and everything, I realized that other than being a medical doctor, I had pretty much fulfilled my ambition of becoming like him. I, too, was a cabinet minister who lectured at the university, worked ridiculously long hours, and constantly traveled across the country delivering public sector services to citizens.

But I still wanted to know how he was able to work as hard as he did after so many decades. "Do it with the right people, David, and it will be fine," he said.

I heard him loudly and clearly.

4

Build a Coalition

· · · · ·

When you speak a language, English, well many
people understand you, including Afrikaners. When
you speak Afrikaans, you know, you go straight to
their hearts.

—NELSON MANDELA

After we've identified a challenge we're passionate about
and understood the role we can play in solving it, the next
question we need to ask ourselves is: Where do we start? For
some challenges, we may be able to proceed alone. But when
it comes to addressing deeply entrenched injustices, we almost
certainly will need help from others. How to get this is seldom
easy or obvious. Not only will we need to figure out how to
identify which people can help us, we also have to work to
get them on board as allies in a coalition to drive change. This

leads us to another important question: Who takes the lead and who must take the back seat in that coalition?

It's important to state from the outset that not everyone can be an ally and, in fact, distinguishing between those who are allies and potential allies and those who aren't is critical to establishing an effective coalition. Further, while we might assume that our acquaintances, friends, family, and mentors will all be allies, this isn't guaranteed. We need to remember that many of our most powerful and important allies will be from far outside our circles and may even be our adversaries at first. Regardless of where our allies originate, finding them, understanding why they would want to join us, and determining what their specific role may be are critical and require real work.

The ability to identify the need for and then establish a coalition is essential, whether you are a leader of an organization or institution or just an ordinary citizen with a desire to change your community in any way and at any scale. Even if you have the power to push through change, a strong, broad-based coalition is almost always necessary for the change to be sustainable.

Coalitions are funny things. Sometimes you build them after a direct confrontation, sometimes they emerge from a shared history or interest, or perhaps they already are in place thanks to an existing relationship like family or mentorship. Sometimes it's as simple as reaching out to an expert whom you enlist to play a very specific role. Some of the strongest coalitions (some might know them as movements) come together organically and are built around ideas.

This chapter presents some tools that I hope will help you build your own coalition or movement on your journey as a changemaker; they were taught to me by mentors I've been lucky enough to encounter on mine.

I went into my first management meeting as minister of education with the goal of sharing my vision with my new team, but it quickly turned into a moment of disappointment, from which I was fortunately able to learn. The conference room was hot, stuffy, and crowded, and filled with a palpable sense of uncertainty. I'd been in it many times before, but never as chair. As I gazed at the familiar cracked paint on the walls and the employees' stony faces, I tried to read their expressions. Was that frown an expression of curiosity or consternation? Was that man's forehead wrinkled because he was wondering whether this new minister would last longer than the eighteen months his predecessor had spent in the role? Was that one thinking that as young as I was I could still do the job, or did he assume I was just another political appointment? Did this other person believe I had something to offer, or did she assume I saw my job as a sinecure?

As for me, I was thinking about how I could mobilize the staff to join me on my mission to transform education.

However long or arduous the journey, if we were to make any progress at all, I needed the help of everyone in that room.

Eager to start my ministerial journey with a bang, I hurriedly told the staff my guiding principles: quality teaching and learning, comprehensive safety, universal access, and radical inclusion. Despite the president's statement at the Freetown International Conference Centre the week before, I also told them that I intended to overturn the ban on pregnant girls in schools. One of the staff interrupted me at that point, saying, "This radical inclusion is a tough one, Minister," flicking a bead of sweat off his face with his index finger and onto the red carpeted floor. His gesture seemed to say, "Did this boy not hear what the president said?"

I took a deep breath and allowed him to finish. He had been a colleague of my mom when she worked in the Bo District education office, so I was careful not to show my impatience. When I resumed talking, I assured him and the other staff that I understood the challenge ahead. I stressed that I was committed to fighting for what the president stood for—accessible quality education for all—and that it was up to us to make that overarching desire a reality. After what I thought was a great introductory statement, I invited all other staff to make comments or ask questions.

There were loud murmurs and then several hands went up. I was shocked at what followed next. Male and female colleagues alike, with no hesitation, told me that most of my ideas would not work. One of them said that he flogs his children at home and thought my plan to enforce the ban on corporal punishment in schools as part of a comprehensive safety framework was bad for society. "Even the Bible says if you spare the rod, you spoil the child and—"

"Thank you, sir," I interrupted. "Not all of us in this room are Christians or even religious. And others of us who are religious do not flog our children." Many more hands were raised, but I continued. "Your point has been noted, but let's try to keep our individual religious beliefs to ourselves next time. Next question?"

One after the other, staff members told me that pregnant girls must not attend school with other students. I corrected them when I thought that their ideas included misinformation, but I was overwhelmed by their negativity. Then one of the assistant directors went a step further. "Sir, this is how these things start. First, we allow pregnant girls in school and before you know it, we will be allowing gays in schools and that can never ever happen here. So, we should stop this right away." I held back my emotions and my anger as his words sank in.

I thought about my gay classmates in Norway and at Harvard who had added so much value to my life. Manuel from Latin America, with whom I spent two years in Norway and then four years in Boston as undergrads—he at MIT and me at Harvard—and how the example of his love, passion, and care had helped me become a better person. I reflected on how he had to battle with his own relatives over his sexual orientation, and ultimately won them over. I thought about John, who also became like a brother to me after four solid years as friends in college, dining, partying, and dancing together with him and his French boyfriend (now married partner). I wondered what would have happened to them if they had not been allowed to attend school because of their sexual orientations. Would I have ever met them and had the benefit of their friendship? Manuel and John have worked in the public sector and academia, and led global consultancies in their short careers, creating services and adding value to society. None of that would have been possible if they had been banned from school.

My assistant Grace beckoned me back to the present with a gesture; the assistant director had finished. I took another deep breath as I formed my response. I would need these people by my side over the long run; I couldn't lose them now before we'd even started. I calmly said, "Maybe someday, our children who are gay can also go freely to school, but that's not what I am asking for now."

The room was as shocked as I was, but for different reasons. This was not a one-day fight, but I recognized that it was a fight. If I was going to be effective as a minister and build a coalition around radical inclusion, I couldn't lose my cool.

That was when it occurred to me that Grace and I were the newest people in the room. Some of them had been in the ministry for more than twenty years; several might have helped draft the policy on which I had just declared war.

But I wasn't going to surrender. It's not only possible to build a coalition through direct confrontation, it's often the best way, provided you clearly state and communicate your principles without getting angry or defensive. Such an approach can embolden those who are inclined to agree but who might otherwise sit silently on the fence, waiting to take a side. Direct engagement also forces those who disagree with you to clearly state why. In doing so, they may come to question their initial position. Engaging in public debate also gives your opponents a public excuse for changing their minds. I had seen that during the town hall in Bombali when Gloria shared her story. It is much easier to avoid public disagreements, but I have found that they can be the bridge that brings our strongest critics over to our side. Still, they're not without risks. And they often require a bit of luck, which I had that day.

In our culture, the oldest people in the room are the most respected, especially if they are women. It helped me greatly that two of the women present at that meeting, Professor Yatta Kanu and Dr. Staneala Beckley—chief education officer and chair of the Teaching Service Commission respectively—were the oldest people in the room; both of them were on my side and said so. Ultimately, the discussion ended with no shift in official positions (this wasn't the expectation anyway), but the tension in the room was tempered. The unspoken sentiment at the beginning had been that this young, new, and inexperienced minister should not come to tell us—seasoned education experts—something that runs against the grain of our culture. As the meeting progressed, more and more members of the staff seemed willing to listen to my views.

I hadn't made much progress, but I had made some and I didn't want to jeopardize it. I drank some water and suggested that we move on to the other items on the agenda.

Grace is not just my executive assistant, she is a trusted confidant and adviser. Prior to returning to Sierra Leone to work for me, she was a feminist activist and one of the most progressive people I knew. I assumed that she and I were on the same wavelength, so when the meeting was over, I called her in to my office to debrief.

I started by expressing how unbelievably wild I thought the conversation had been at the beginning, and how disappointed I was that I hadn't made more headway. Grace has opinions about everything, and she is happy to share them, even when not asked. But that day she was uncharacteristically quiet.

"What is it, Grace?" I asked.

She flipped her long hair weaves back, revealing her entire face. "Sir, I agree with some of what the staff were saying," she said. "I don't think schoolgirls who are pregnant should stay in the same classrooms with non-pregnant girls." She began to explain herself, but I was too shocked and surprised to follow her reasoning.

I stared at the large painting on my wall. It was a portrait, rendered in black and white, of Madam Ella Koblo Gulama, the first woman parliamentarian in Sierra Leone, and the first woman cabinet minister in sub-Saharan Africa. I'd bought it at an event organized by a civil society group called Power Women 232. After she left the government, Madam Gulama would go on to become a local leader and paramount chief. I'd hung the picture as an inspiration and role model for me and anyone who entered my office, including Grace. I looked at Grace and back at the painting and then back at Grace, and I couldn't understand how it was possible that she and I could be so far apart on a topic related to gender empowerment. As the reality of not having my staff or even Grace on my side dawned on me, she yanked me out of my emotional whirlwind by saying:

"Sir, listen: my sister was born before my mother completed her secondary school education. In between her O Level and A Level examinations, she gave birth to my sister. . . ."

I listened carefully to Grace's story. Now I understood how she had come to her opinion. Still, I was convinced she was wrong. Then I had an idea.

Grace's mother, Aunty Rhoda, was highly educated; she was at the time one of the most senior civil servants in the Human Resource Management Organization. I encouraged Grace to ask her what she thought of the ban. Although she was over eighteen at the time of her pregnancy, how did being a parent learner affect her in school? What did she think today? I knew Grace was devoted to her family and her religion, and suspected that if anyone could change her mind about something she believed to be a moral and religious matter, it would be her mother. I didn't know Aunty Rhoda's position on the topic (and in that conversation, Grace mentioned that she and her mother had not had any deep conversations about this in the past), but I figured it was worth a chance. At that moment the power failed, killing the lights and the air conditioner. It provided a natural ending to our conversation and an opportunity for me to think things through.

In addition to underestimating the work of identifying and establishing a strong coalition, I'd also, naïvely perhaps, assumed that those closest to me professionally would be my allies. Somehow, I would have to figure out how to assemble a coalition that was willing to fight alongside me. I needed to come up with some principles to help me do this. I went back to my past to try to recall any lessons from people I had met and admired, and to see what mistakes I'd made that shouldn't be repeated.

The boundary between friends and family was very thin when I was growing up in Bo. In addition to sheltering my nuclear family, our house was the permanent residence of a large group of extended family. It also included any number of my brothers' friends who had come to visit and then wound up moving in. It was a simple process. One day they'd stay for dinner and then join us to watch a Jackie Chan movie in the living room. By the time it was over, it would be too late for them to go home, if they had not fallen asleep already. A few days later, they would come over again and do the same thing. This soon became a pattern, and after a while they would show up at our house with a suitcase and settle in. At various points in my childhood as many as ten young boys shared the same sleeping rooms with us. We'd sleep three to a bed with the others on mats on the floor. This was still more comfortable than some of the homes they came from. It was never really clear which friends were permanently in our home and which were just spending a few nights, but my parents would take full responsibility for the school fees and other needs of anyone who stayed on, and they never expected anything in return.

When Bo came under attack during the civil war, our family had to flee under gunfire. My grandmother, Mama Bee, who lived with us at the time, was old, obese, and walked gingerly with a cane. As everyone packed their belongings, some food, and any necessary personal documents, the question of how we would run with Mama Bee loomed, as her staying in Bo was not an option. This was when the young, strong boys in the house decided that they would take turns carrying her on their backs, swapping her periodically by the side of the road as thousands of other families walked past us. Between our departure at about 5:30 A.M. and our arrival after midnight in the village we settled in, my brothers, cousins, and their friends effortlessly worked together, ensuring that we all reached safety. As a group, they led us through unknown territories, made jokes that lightened our burdens, and kept our family together.

To this day, it's one of the most powerful coalitions I've ever witnessed. Thinking back on it, it reminded me of the power of family—and that we get to define our families as we see fit. When we are there for others, there is a much higher chance they will be there for us. Natural coalitions that evolve organically are the most powerful. Of course, you can't simply will a coalition into being at a new workplace, in a new neighborhood, or across geographic boundaries.

Then I thought back to times I had received crucial help from those outside my family—acquaintances, friends, allies, and mentors.

My childhood friend Martha Sellu—who passed away from sickle cell anemia while I was in college—and I used to discuss our teenage challenges, including our romantic interests. Martha was soft-spoken and had a gentle laugh; even as she endured severe pain during her illness, she knew how to bring joy to others. I often still channel the curious sets of questions she would ask in order to understand a situation better before sharing her perspectives. "What is the real problem here, Moinina?" she would ask. "What's in it for you and what's in it for them?" and "Why does it matter?" These questions, always asked with empathy and love, help clarify the essence of our relationships with others. They also establish the expectations of all the parties in a coalition. From Martha, I learned that for a coalition to be effective, every party within it has to be satisfied.

This is something Bill Carrier would also teach me many years later. Bill, who has been my leadership coach for eight years, introduced me to something he calls the "anatomy of actions," a crucial tool I have used throughout my journey from graduate student to manager at a private sector institution and then cabinet minister. The first principle is to listen to people, to understand what they truly care about. Then you should have a conversation with them that helps them make a commitment to take the actions that will get the outcomes you and they desire. It is not a manipulative tool, even if it sounds like it; rather, it allows us to engage others and ensure that we are working together toward an explicitly stated set of objectives.

Samzu has been one of my closest friends since junior secondary school. Whether we are walking through dusty byroads together in Freetown or visiting museums in London, we never run out of things to say and we share a history of unconventional problem-solving. Once, we were caught swimming in the ocean and were immediately suspended from school. Knowing our parents would not take our suspensions lightly, we recruited a stranger off the street and paid him to pretend to be our uncle. It was important our parents not hear of our suspension from any family member. We were still flogged, and our "uncle" played his part a bit too well; he joined in and caned us, too, before asking for pardon on our behalf. This didn't deter us from learning how to swim; we saved our lunch money so we could pay for swimming lessons at the National Stadium. Whether as the first listener to a new rap lyric I've composed or the first reader of a draft opinion piece, I can always trust Samzu to give me his unfiltered opinion.

I should add that after we have hashed out a problem together, Samzu always becomes a champion of our position, even when he's not involved in direct action. Not everyone that helps you achieve a mission has to be on the front lines with you. But you do need people with whom you can stress-test your ideas, who you can trust to tell you in private what you may not want to hear, and to defend you and your ideas in public when you may not be in the room.

Martha and Samzu were peers, and Bill is a friend as much as a coach. I next thought about teachers who taught me about building coalitions. The first that came to mind was David Edwards, one of my professors at Harvard.

After completing my secondary school education but before matriculating at Harvard, I began to think about the causes in Sierra Leone I could use my education to further. In August 2006, I visited a center for amputees in Freetown where they made prosthetic devices. Sierra Leone had tens of thousands of amputees as a result of the civil war; many were beggars on the street. When I asked if there was anything I could do to help, everyone told me that one of the biggest problems was that the prostheses were not comfortable, especially for growing children. I emailed a set of professors asking for their mentorship and support to address this challenge. I didn't know it at the time, but it was one of my first attempts at coalition-building.

Two weeks after I arrived at Harvard, Professor Edwards offered me a space in his lab and kept it open for the next four years; in fact, our relationship remains strong to this day. David showed me that with the right set of partners, nothing is impossible. In 2008, when I was still an undergraduate, he helped me and several collaborators win more than $200,000 in grants from the World Bank to develop and deploy microbial fuel cells in Namibia. In the years since, I've seen David develop inhalable vaccines in his labs in Paris and Boston, and admired his progress on a multitude of start-ups. In order to achieve all the things he has, he had to enlist allies from all disciplines, sectors, and walks of life. He is not only drawn to good ideas, but invests resources and energy in cultivating good people. From David I learned that it's never too early to draft someone into a coalition, because he took a chance on me when I had absolutely nothing to offer in return.

After graduating from Harvard, I joined the MIT Media Lab to pursue my PhD research on the design of prosthetic sockets with Professor Hugh Herr. My research was at the intersection of several emerging fields; evaluation of my designs involved active collaborations with prosthetists, medical imaging physicists, soft tissue modeling experts, and companies that manufacture 3-D printers, as well as clinical trials with patients. In my pursuit of the best, I sought out and approached companies that care about comfort, like the shoe company New Balance, and research scientists whose names I only knew of from academic journals.

Kevin Moerman, a Dutch postdoctoral researcher then based at the Amsterdam University Medical Center, replied to one of my emails. Kevin had developed an open-source toolkit for soft tissue model development and evaluation, and was looking for collaborators who could apply his codebase to different applications. He opened his entire portfolio to me, starting up a multi-year collaboration. As my friend Martha would have pointed out, we found out what was in it for each of us. Two weeks after Kevin and his wife had their second baby, I was in their home in the Netherlands at their invitation, working on developing custom code for prosthetic socket design using his tools. Between babysitting, taking long walks in community markets, and biking with their three-year-old son, we would code late into the night, periodically pausing to share a glass of wine or a pint of locally brewed beer. The shapes of flowers on ponds that we'd see during our walks would often give us ideas for how to achieve variable compliance in our socket designs. Both of us shared the goal of solving an intractable problem that could improve the lives of millions of amputees; beyond that, we found that we could promote and elevate each other's work.

After I returned to Cambridge, Kevin and I enhanced our collaboration, working regularly through Skype and other virtual interfaces. We would even take remote control of each other's computers as needed, often to the astonishment of my lab colleagues with whom I shared an office. Less than a year later, Kevin and his family moved to MIT. Perhaps unsurprisingly, Kevin joined Hugh on my thesis committee supervising my research, which developed a first-of-its-kind solution that one of my patients said was not only comfortable, but "effing sexy."

While our initial contact was driven by an interest in each other's work, Kevin and I built a true friendship. We would argue long into the evening about theories and designs as we patiently waited for modeling simulation runs that often took hours to complete. When we took our families to neighborhood markets around the Boston area, it was not uncommon for one of us to pick up a twig and draw equations on the ground as we worked out aspects of what would be our shared patents.

David taught me how to keep the big vision in perspective and Kevin taught me to focus on the detailed technical work required to drive change. Hugh created the platform for change to happen at all levels. By being my PhD adviser and mentor, and also offering his body, literally, as a double amputee, for us to experiment on, we were able to do something profound.

Back in Sierra Leone, I would need to put all of these lessons to use. I tried my best to do so. But there was yet another challenge. Not only was I not a teacher or mentor of the people I most needed to enlist, I wasn't even their peer.

When I first joined the office of the president as chief innovation officer in 2018, I was considerably younger than many of my colleagues. Since our culture is hierarchical and very respectful of the elderly, it was challenging for me to build deep relationships with many of my much older colleagues. This was even harder because some were literally my uncles and aunties who'd known me as a child.

One exception was Dr. Patrick K. Muana. Widely known as PK, Dr. Muana serves as a senior presidential adviser for strategic communications. He, like me, returned to Sierra Leone from academia and research. Unlike many other experts from the social sciences or arts I have met in government, PK loves data and loves to walk the untrodden path—a path I would always choose to walk alongside him, and not just because of our shared love for brightly colored patterned socks!

The president, PK, and I built a very open and transparent relationship that allowed us to talk freely about everything, from talking points for events and ways to problem-solve sticky governance issues to new ideas. The day the president publicly supported the ban on pregnant girls, PK was the first person I called. When I told him that ending it might prove to be an impossible task for me, he burst into laughter and, switching to Mende, told me to "relax." I observed that his choice of language depended on what he wanted to get across. He used our mother tongue when he wanted to create a deeper connection upon which to build my confidence. PK's reassurance during that call meant a lot to me; his calm can be infectious. Perhaps it is because he is a karateka (a 7th dan black belt in Shotokan karate) who has trained all over the world for decades, including in Japan.

After that eye-opening conversation at the ministry with my staff and then with Grace, and after recalling the lessons from my various friends and mentors, I called PK again. Right away, he told me to head over to his office at the State House.

Every time I enter his office, which has a big DO NOT KNOCK sign on its door, PK welcomes me with a broad smile, revealing his perfectly white teeth. No matter the complexity of the problems I bring him, I immediately feel at ease in his presence.

He asked me how I proposed to bring about the lifting of the ban. I paused and said, "Well, it has to pass through cabinet first. The president has to turn back on his words." He laughed off my statement and walked toward a whiteboard on the wall, where he began mapping all the stakeholders within and outside government that would have to be convinced first. In addition to strong individual allies like PK, the coalition of the willing would have to include friends and family; colleagues within the ministry and across the government; civil society and religious groups; development partners; and most important, the public.

I thought back to Martha, Samzu, Bill, and my various professors, all of whom taught me aspects of how to engage with individuals to bring them into a coalition. But here was one of the most valuable lessons of all—the need for a strategy.

PK, a former professor of English and communications at Texas A&M University, was teaching me that to set up an effective coalition, I needed to map it fully, specifying clear roles for each ally. He sounded like a professor, and I was his willing student.

My final lesson in coalition-building came from my boss, President Bio. The irony that I would use his lesson to try to reverse one of his own positions was not lost on me.

President Bio served as a military leader in his previous professional life, fighting in Sierra Leone's civil war as an officer and later the commander of the army. He would rise to head of state and, in 1996, help transition the country from military to democratic rule. Over meals, he often shares detailed and expansive lessons from the front lines, including the strategies he used in combat, in the military barracks, and at the negotiating table when he signed Sierra Leone's peace accords with the rebels. Every leadership manual speaks about the influence of generals in war, but no battle can be won without an army. President Bio taught me that a military coup can be successful only when and if the people want it. He led two coups in his life, and they were successful because he knew they were good for the people, and that the people themselves wanted the change, even if they perhaps did not know it or know how to express it.

Overturning the ban on pregnant girls was not unlike a coup. As the cabinet minister and general in charge, I would have to build an army of champions using all the tools I had learned. But did the people want it? Did they even know about the policy and its influence?

To find out, I checked the pulse of society the way I always do, at the dinner table at home.

My wife, Kate, was on my team from the start. She is one of the first people I engage with on almost every matter of interest to me. We don't always start from the same place because of our different backgrounds (she's an atheist, I am Catholic; she's white, I am Black; she's American, I am Sierra Leonean, etc.), nor do we often end in the same place, but we always end up in a more refined position than the one from which we started. This time, though, she was with me from the start and ever more fervently. What I was curious about was whether I had managed to convince my niece Kadija.

I soon learned that I finally had. Several weeks into my public engagements on the topic, Kadija announced that she'd considered the question a bit more and updated her position. In fact, she had completely changed her mind. I asked her how that had happened. "Well, I listened to your arguments and I agree with you and the president that everyone should go to school." She explained then that if you believed that everyone meant everyone, then that really should mean *everyone*. Previously, she explained, she had been worried about the health and performance of pregnant girls in school. She also worried that they would be bullied. But since she now had assurances based on my public engagements that they would get more support, then those girls should indeed be allowed to attend school. She also indicated that she didn't think she herself would want to get pregnant just because a schoolmate had. Every person's situation was different, she told me.

I smiled, hugged her, and continued my meal. There are some issues that people just can't change their minds about. This wasn't one of them. In fact, Kadija became an ardent campaigner for lifting the ban.

Motivated by her change of mind and heart, I engaged

everyone in my household and my extended family on this issue—something I had neglected to do initially. I rang my mom, dad, sister, brothers, and anyone else who was willing to listen. It was only then that I learned that many of my family members had also supported the ban.

My sister, always frank, told me she reckoned that I was thinking like an outsider because I had lived abroad, and that the majority of the public was firmly in favor of the ban. Using the trick I'd learned from PK, I answered her in Mende to drive home the message that I was as Sierra Leonean as she is. As Nelson Mandela once advised, "When you speak a language, English, well many people understand you, including Afrikaners. When you speak Afrikaans, you know, you go straight to their hearts." My brothers are generally liberal but can be quite conservative on topics they believe conflict with Catholicism, so I talked to their hearts independently and as a group, testing old and new arguments on them, noting carefully which approaches seemed to work and which didn't. I learned from these and many other difficult conversations that what got people to change their perspectives was thinking about their own daughters, or, if they didn't have daughters, when I asked them to imagine they did.

Empathy always improves our understanding, but it does so particularly when the issues are complex. I used my nieces as examples with my sister and brothers, and I also asked them to imagine if they were the children in question. What would happen if Kadija got pregnant in school? "No, my child would never get pregnant," my sister replied.

After a long silence, we then explored the different scenarios in which Kadija would be loved and supported. At some point, my sister relaxed her rigid stance, and by the end, she became a champion of inclusion, telling me that she would want Kadija to be able to continue her education no matter what.

Empathy breaks barriers, and quickly. And barriers must be broken to form strong coalitions. It is the most powerful tool a leader can have. No matter how much I disagree with someone, no matter how wrong I think their comments are, whether in person or online, I always pause for a minute and allow myself to imagine the emotions that underpin and drive their experience, whether they are my friend or not.

Using the tools of my friends and mentors, I had enlisted my family in my coalition. Now it was time to expand it. For leaders and social changemakers today, building coalitions online is as important, if not more so, than doing it in person. Barack Obama and Greta Thunberg are very good examples of leaders who successfully leveraged their social media platforms to broaden their bases, build movements, and establish permanent allies across the world for their causes.

I intensified my public engagements and doubled down

on my use of traditional and online media. This was part of the original plan PK had helped me outline on the whiteboards in his office. There were periods when I was either on the radio or TV every week to discuss different aspects of education, but I always found a way to insert the topic of pregnant girls in school. They were often difficult conversations, but I was prepared for them because I'd had similarly tough conversations with family and friends.

Just as when I'd appeared on *Good Morning Salone,* many of the hosts of the popular talk shows were dead set against the idea of including pregnant girls in school. The questions they directed at me sought to counter my arguments before I even had an opportunity to speak. I felt attacked, especially when the hosts cherry-picked comments and questions from members of the public who were also against my position. But I valued those moments, too, because they gave me an opportunity to counter people's fears and myths using data and evidence. The only way to change someone's mind is by allowing them to express their fears and ideas, and then engaging with them with empathy and honesty.

Granted, this comes at a cost. A personal emotional cost that can be detrimental if not managed well. Every time I left a radio or television studio, I would continue engaging online on Facebook and in private WhatsApp groups. Hiding behind two-dimensional black-and-white texts, some of my online adversaries directed the most vile and hateful comments at me. If they were not cursing the government or cursing me, they would be calling for me to be fired because I'd learned the ways of the white man and the devil on my travels abroad. "This is not America!" they would remind me. The irony was that so many of them were based in either Europe or America themselves.

Nevertheless, I engaged with as many people as I could, staying up late into the night. My parents and friends worried for my mental health and urged me to disengage. At some points it did become too much, and I would suspend my social media accounts for a while—one natural time was during the period of Lent. But I always returned in time.

While social media is a powerful tool for building coalitions that transcend borders and expand our reach in nonlinear ways, it can also be profoundly damaging. It propagates misinformation as widely as facts do—if not more so. There is always the risk that those platforms can be used to derail or undermine your work. But as I see it, this is precisely the reason to be active on them—you and your team are the best people to correct misinformation. And one of the best ways to correct misinformation is to provide the correct information without directly amplifying the misinformation yourself. When you are identified as a credible source of information, people begin to follow you and wait for your input before drawing any conclusions. This is how you can expand a credible coalition online.

After months of engaging online and offline, some of my fiercest opponents began to yield. The coalition was expanding, and I would now read comments in which young people I didn't know were repeating arguments I'd made on the radio or on social media. I no longer needed to reply to every comment, as someone else would. While some of my fiercest opponents (religious, political, or cultural-based groups) remained staunchly entrenched in their views, I now had recruits who could continue the work of softening them while I focused on other segments of the population.

Several of our critical partners were global donors and funders of education. The European Union, the World Bank, UNICEF, Irish Aid, and the Foreign, Commonwealth and Development Office (formerly DFID) had all been actively lobbying for the government to lift the ban since long before I became a minister. Initially, they were direct and confrontational, which was counterproductive. But after we started to get traction with public opinion, I met with the heads of those organizations, thanked them for their help, and asked them to take a back seat in the fight. As important a piece of the coalition as they were, they could not lead it.

Again, this drew on all I had learned from my mentors and the plan PK had helped me design. Many cabinet members and civil society leaders were already suspicious about the underlying agenda of these global NGOs. For as long as they remained the face of the fight for inclusion, the president would resist, certain they were trying to bully us and dictate an agenda for our sovereign nation. I explained these challenges and reminded them that while we were all on the same team, my ministry and I would need to do all the talking. They did not object because they were committed to the cause and realized that the message is more important than the messenger.

Then I invited all those donor and development partners to form a consortium with us. As it came together, the ministry was able to establish a special task force that included many different kinds of stakeholders. That is the crucial next step for creating change. You start with individuals representing themselves, but you need to move on to people who speak for and can marshal broader groups. The task force could commission and undertake relevant research, develop white papers, draft policy documents, and serve as a platform for engaging civil society and the community.

I tried to join as many of those meetings as possible so I could help clarify any issues as they came up. In the beginning, I spent a huge chunk of time explaining what I meant by the term 'radical inclusion' and discussing the scope of the policy on radical inclusion in schools. Radical inclusion means more than ensuring access to schooling for girls irrespective of their reproductive status—it means making sure that *everyone* can go to school, including those segments of the population who were typically absent for some or part of the year.

I explained that our objective was to include all persons directly or indirectly excluded due to any set of actions or inactions. Such exclusions could emanate from government policies, the infrastructure designs of government, society, and religion, or our collective silence in the face of systemic inequities. Radical inclusion, I continued, means that all such exclusionary policies, moral stances, and systemic frameworks should be removed intentionally, so that every child can access and stay safely in school.

The member organizations all had different central interests as defined by their mission statements, and they often had a narrow focus. My role was to keep the debates expansive. Even within a coalition—perhaps especially within a coalition—intersectionality can exist. The chances that members would achieve their own individual interests and priorities improved within a coalition, which was reason enough for joining one. I think this is the most important thing about coalitions and indeed about radical inclusion itself. It's most powerful when it's most expansive, when there is a whole environment built around making sure that everyone has an equal opportunity to win.

Ultimately, the task force was able to develop an excellent

research document and position paper on the issue of girls' education. They supported the inclusion of sexual and reproductive health in the curriculum developed by the ministry, a big step forward. Most important, it was unanimous in favor of pregnant girls and parent learners attending school. The task force members presented this view irrespective of their personal views. In fact, prior to seeing the final documents, the parliamentarian representative on the task force visited my office to tell me that while she personally had her doubts, she believed in the task force's work. She believed in me, she said, and was fully prepared to engage the rest of the Parliament in support of the inclusion of pregnant girls in schools, if and when the government so desired. I respected her for that and thanked her and told her that Madam Ella Koblo Gulama must be smiling in her grave (both come from the same district).

Right around that time, Grace asked to speak to me. She told me she'd had a series of conversations with her mother and her sister—the one who was born while her mother was in school—and had "updated" her position on the matter as a result. She now believed that pregnant girls should indeed go to school.

Thanks to our coalition-building, I had been able to form a task force at the right time and with the right people, which had issued a paper that I could now take to the cabinet. But my most important test still lay ahead, which was to convince the cabinet.

The cabinet became the most important member of the coalition; without its recommendation, I wouldn't have a chance. The paper I had would certainly help. But even with it, I had reason to believe that the road ahead was going to be incredibly difficult. Immediately prior to my appointment as minister in September 2019, I had traveled with several cabinet members to the United Nations General Assembly. While waiting in the airport lounge in Paris, I asked a cross section of them what they thought about lifting the ban and to my horror, they were all against it. When I say all of them, I should add that the cabinet colleagues included two former ministers of education. When I tried to engage further, I was advised not to push it, that it would be politically unwise.

After we paused the conversation, I put another warm chocolate croissant on my plate and washed it down with a gulp of cold orange juice. Then I took out my headphones and hit play on an Afrobeat playlist that was in sync with the increased tempo of my heartbeat.

When we were on the plane and the flight attendant asked me to remove my headphones as we prepared to take off, I tapped one of the ministers on the shoulder and asked, "Do you really believe pregnant girls can be a bad influence on other girls in school?" She smiled and replied in Krio, *"Bo*

David lef mi bo." The emotion behind this expression of ridicule does not translate well, but what comes closest is, "David, please leave me alone, not even worth discussing." I quickly put my headphones back on after we took off.

Several months had passed since then. Sure, we had the data, and, over a period of time, had built a coalition of acquaintances, friends, families, mentors, and even some former opponents. We had brought together and gained agreement from individuals representing various groups and constituencies, domestic and global. Thanks to the conversations Grace had with her mother, she was now on our side. But none of that would matter if I couldn't convince the cabinet.

Imagine you've seen an injustice in your own workplace and that you and some of your colleagues have mobilized around an effort to end it. You would undertake a broad range of initiatives, including informal lunch dialogues, maybe even writing and sharing a compelling report based on original research. But until you can convince the decision makers in your organization's C-suite, no permanent change will happen. For systemic change, a strong coalition has far more chance of succeeding than any individual. But even a very strong coalition can fail.

So it was time that I exercised some different muscles.

5

Advocacy and Action

. . . . .

If you had / One shot, or one opportunity / To seize
everything you ever wanted / One moment / Would
you capture it or just let it slip?

—EMINEM, "LOSE YOURSELF"

I was at my desk in my State House office, leaning back in my leather-covered swivel chair with my headphones on, when my phone started to buzz. It was Wednesday morning, which is always blocked off in my calendar for cabinet meetings. That day, I was to present three items on the agenda. Two were straightforward, but I was quite nervous and unsure about the third. With the noise-canceling feature on the headphones on and my eyes closed, I was listening to Eminem: "You only get one shot, do not miss your chance to blow / This opportunity comes once in a lifetime / You better lose yourself in the music. . . ."

As I prepared myself to capture the moment, my mind raced back in time to the Bo town hall where a rap battle was taking place. I was ten years old. It was one in the morning and I was the next to go up on stage, alongside my eldest brother and his teenage friends. My favorite artists back then were Tupac Shakur and Biggie Smalls—two of the best hip-hop artists ever. While my mother knew I rapped, she definitely did not know I had memorized many of their age-inappropriate lyrics which shared their stories of trials, tribulations, and success, inviting their fans into a fantasy world where everything was possible.

To channel their energy and shut out the noise of the crowd, I would listen to their hit singles right before I went on stage. Once I was on stage, nothing else mattered. I was walking on air and I could see the faces of every fan through the blinding stage lights. I spat out my lines effortlessly because I'd written them and had practiced them ad nauseam at home with my friends in between playing football and doing chores, watering the family's potato and cassava gardens. When I came back to earth at the end of the performance I would be completely drained but filled with utter joy and satisfaction. Football is the only other activity apart from music that can occupy my mind so fully, leaving no room for distracting thoughts. But I can't just pull out a ball and juggle it in the office.

I still turn to rap music to calm my nerves before stressful meetings and presentations, but it does far more for me than that; it's how I get into and stay in focus. It reminds me how good it feels to give something you care about your total and complete attention. When my phone kept buzzing, I opened my eyes, squinting against the bright sunlight reflecting off the roofs of the colorful houses that line the hills along Freetown's southern axis. My office is in the west wing of the State House; it looks out across the hills, the city, and the ocean. The name Sierra Leone is from the Portuguese *serra loya,* meaning "lion mountains." The folklore is that the first European to sight and map the Freetown harbor named the country after its beautiful mountains.

"Minister, it is ten fifty, where are you? The vice president is about to enter the cabinet room," said one of the staff of the cabinet secretariat when I finally answered the phone. Typically, the vice president and the president are the last two people to enter the cabinet room and after that, the doors are closed. "Holy cannoli!" I gasped. "I'll be right there."

I grabbed my red notepad and the bulky yellow envelope marked SECRET which contained all the cabinet documents for the day. I also took a folder that included some extra materials Grace had put together, including a summary brief prepared by the Sexual and Reproductive Taskforce we had established and the declaration from a ruling by the Economic Community of West African States Court of Justice on December 12, 2019, which found the ban on pregnant girls in schools to be in violation of their right to an education. "The Court found the government of Sierra Leone to be in breach of Articles 2, 3, 17, 18, 25 of the African Charter; Articles 21 and 28a of the Convention on the Rights of the Child, and Articles 1 and 3 of the Convention Against Discrimination in Education," it read in part.

I ran down the State House's magnificent spiral staircase, past the entrance to the president's suite on the second floor, and down to the first floor where the cabinet room is located. Typically, I stop to give fist bumps and have casual conversations with security staff, but this time, I returned their greetings of "Mr. Minister, morning, sir" with just a wave. I made it just moments before the vice president entered the room.

Out of breath, I said hello to some of my fellow ministers. One of them leaned in toward me and whispered, "David, are you really sure you want pregnant girls in schools?" I smiled a bit awkwardly, but before I could respond, the giant wooden doors at the back of the room opened wide. The state chief of protocol walked in and with his familiar booming but calm intonation announced, "Ladies and gentlemen, His

Excellency the president." We all stood up as the president made his entrance. Usually he would give me a slight nod as he passed my seat, but it was different that day. I couldn't look at him directly and I don't think he acknowledged me. I still had no clarity on what the president's final position on the topic was.

I had learned a lot about how to make radical inclusion a reality. I had recognized an exclusion, learned as much as I could about it on my own, listened to those who had been excluded tell me their challenges and hopes, and spoken with the excluders. I had worked to find allies—not just ones whose interests overlapped totally with mine but also people and groups who saw this as a way of advancing other causes that were even more important to them.

But all of that would come to naught if the cabinet did not support me. Only the cabinet could overturn the ban, as it had been put in place by a previous cabinet of government. While I didn't expect every cabinet member to be on my side, I hoped to win over a few more of those that were on the fence. Silence would not be golden—colleagues would have to make their voices heard in favor of the memorandum if we were to reach a consensus on it during the debate.

The topic of lifting the ban on pregnant girls in schools had been added to the agenda in the first place only because I had followed the playbook of one of my most valued mentors, Jakaya Kikwete, the former president of Tanzania. Our relationship goes back only a couple of years; we met at a leadership program in South Africa in 2018 and again at the African Union Summit in Addis Ababa in early 2020, just a few weeks before this cabinet meeting. On that second occasion, I asked him some pointed questions.

"*Mzee,* as president, what were the attributes you found most productive in your high-performing ministers? What made you support seemingly impossible and difficult decisions in cabinet meetings?"

President Kikwete paused, reflecting before he answered. When he did begin to speak, he was interrupted by another former president who had stopped to exchange pleasantries. I thought that would be the end of my free leadership consultation. But when they finished, President Kikwete turned back to me and looked directly into my eyes. "I was always most pleased when my ministers brought to me their policies for discussion prior to presenting them at cabinet," he said. "Ministers must understand that the president is busy, but that said, they must still seek his input into all policy development. The president knows a lot more than people think and he wants to be consulted, especially on difficult decisions before they are fully developed. I mean, if things don't work, the president is the one who is booted out." I took out my notebook and jotted down his words. "As a minister, you do not want the president to be the one to say 'no' to your cabinet paper," he concluded.

I did not wait to act on his advice. That evening, over dinner with President Bio in his hotel room, I told him I was going to bring a difficult paper to cabinet. He looked up from his food when I said it was about reversing the ban on pregnant girls, but he didn't say anything or express any emotion. Another cabinet minister was also at the table. She's a good friend, and I knew she was not yet on my side. She moved awkwardly in her chair, like she wanted to say something, but I didn't acknowledge her. I did not want her to share her views at this time.

The awkward silence reverberated in the room while President Bio finished his mouthful. Then he lifted his head again and said, "Sure, we will discuss it in Freetown." While I did not know whether his opinion had softened or changed, his willingness to discuss it felt like a big win for me. The state chief of protocol came into the room a few minutes later, and I asked him to schedule a private meeting for me with the president as soon as we returned to Sierra Leone.

When I entered the president's office on the day of the meeting, he got up to run the coffee maker. I glanced across the room and noticed he had reorganized the medals and tchotchkes on the book cabinet behind his desk. He asked about my family as he handed me a cup. Nyaanina was growing up fast, I said. I asked about Amina—his daughter who is a year older than Nyaanina. Then we spent some time discussing general governance issues. Finally I said, "Your excellency, I am ready to bring to cabinet a memorandum asking government to overturn the ban on pregnant girls attending school. Sir, I would like your permission to bring the paper directly to cabinet and not first to subcommittee." I told him that after several discussions with my colleagues, I didn't think they would even debate the topic at the subcommittee meeting, never mind support it. The topic required his direct input because he had taken a public stance in opposition to it.

What was meant to be a brief meeting turned into an extended discussion. We began talking about a book that President Bio and I both admire, *No Room for Small Dreams,* the autobiography of Israel's former president and prime minister Shimon Peres. Peres never hesitated to project strength but was also willing to negotiate, and combined daring innovation with straightforward pragmatism. In his book he shared several instances when, in defiance of the conventional wisdom, he was able to convince his colleagues and the nation to believe and do things that were thought impossible. Peres not only helped create Israel's ambitious nuclear energy program, but seeded its high-tech revolution with Start-Up Nation Central.

As we talked about his stories of grit, resilience, and perseverance, it was not lost on either of us that many of the most important agreements in government are reached outside the cabinet room, during bilateral discussions with key individuals.

Reflecting on the Israel-Egypt War, Peres stated:

It was, for me personally, a time of profound development—a time when wisdom was formed under extraordinary pressure. . . . We were quick and creative, and boldly ambitious, and in that we found our reward. But I also learned that there is a cost to dreaming. At first it was my ideas that were ridiculed. Soon, however, it was me—and only by extension, my positions—who took most of the incoming fire. . . . And because so much of what I did was in secret . . . I had little choice but to live in the shadows. My critics often knew—and would only ever know—half the story. In this, I came to understand the choice at the heart of leadership: to pursue big dreams and suffer the consequences, or narrow one's ambitions in an effort to get along.

Peres had been a young leader—he was still in his twenties when he became director general of defense. The first prime minister of Israel, David Ben-Gurion, had been his most important mentor. But Peres didn't take no for an answer easily, even from his mentors. From his days as a young activist, he always spoke up for the things he believed in, and was steadfast when they met resistance. Like Ben-Gurion and Peres, like Bio and Sengeh, I thought.

One of the main things Peres is known for is the role he played in Operation Entebbe. Air France flight 139 from Tel Aviv had been hijacked and was being held on the tarmac at Entebbe International Airport in Uganda. Though the terrorists released 148 non-Israeli passengers, ninety-four Israeli passengers and the twelve-person flight crew were still hostages. Peres, who was minister of defense at the time, felt there was just one option—military action. At first, he "was the only one in the room" who believed it might work, but after a series of consultations he pushed his proposal for the risky operation through. Peres reflects that a large lesson from Entebbe was that "without emboldening people to envisage the unlikely, we increase risk rather than diminish it."

President Bio and I agreed that Peres's uncanny sense of strength and purpose, along with his coalition-building and the willingness to negotiate, should be a model for us as we attempted to shape the future of Sierra Leone. More than anything, Peres had dared to dream.

Though I still didn't know where President Bio stood on the question of pregnant schoolgirls, he granted me his approval to bring the memorandum directly to cabinet. The rest was up to me. I hoped I would be able to summon some of Peres's spirit to push it through. I, too, would dare to dream.

I understood the risks. The proposal might have been tabled indefinitely or rejected out of hand in subcommittee, and I would have missed an opportunity to learn all of my opponents' arguments. But I got lucky—and luck is a very important ingredient of leadership—when an opportunity to build a coalition with supporters and learn my adversaries' arguments outside the subcommittee room presented itself just a few days before the meeting. As it happened, the president and the first lady were hosting a dinner at their residence in celebration of a state guest, and almost all of the cabinet and deputy ministers were invited.

While the real action and debate would happen in the cabinet room, the work I could do at the dinner was equally important. Decisive action takes different forms and can happen in different locations. Some opportunities we plan for and others are granted to us by mother luck, but no matter how they appear, we must be ready. As changemakers, we must always be on the lookout for serendipity. Louis Pasteur famously said, "Chance favors only the prepared mind," and I was not going to let this chance get away from me.

I arrived at the dinner early, and didn't waste any time with idle chatter—instead, I asked each of my colleagues directly about their position on the ban. Standing on the green lawn in front of the president's residence with drinks in hand, one after the other—men and women, young and old—told me they would not support overturning the ban.

I probed them about the reasons for their objections so I could find an appropriate response for each. It's important that you study your opponents' offense, so you can develop a strong defense. But it can help you plan your attack as well. I did not have my notebook on me (although I'm known as the "digital minister" among my colleagues, I usually carry a pen and a colorful notebook so I can jot down ideas, questions, thoughts, and summaries of meetings) so I wrote my notes on the back of the dinner invitation.

I was feeling pretty low until I began chatting with the deputy minister of social welfare. He immediately announced himself as an ally and took on the role of bad cop with my colleagues, haranguing them until some agreed to come over to our side. Still, when we sat down for dinner in the cool evening breeze, I was anything but relaxed. You should never go into battle without knowing you have the resources and the allies you need. But it had been such an arduous journey to get to where we were that I didn't dare to pause the process. Should my proposal fall off the agenda, it might not ever get back on it again.

And now I was at the crucial meeting, sweating and out of breath from my run to the cabinet room, waiting for my

turn on the agenda. For any major speech, program, or event
I have attended over the last decade, I've worn a shirt either
my mother or I designed. That morning I chose one that we'd
created together—I felt that I needed her energy around me.
I was also wearing some nice dress pants complemented by a
pair of bold orange socks. And, as a practicing Catholic, I had
my rosary beads.

If you are going into battle, it helps to have the right ar-
mor.

No matter what happened, I told myself, this is only the
beginning of the fight to achieve universal education. Even
though the cabinet debate centered around a couple of thousand pregnant girls, its outcome would be important for the
millions of girls in school today and in the future—in Sierra
Leone, and in all the other countries that still ban pregnant
girls from school.

The president struck the table with the gavel to begin.
There were prayers, followed by the national pledge and
then the president's opening statements, which focused on
national transformation. As he spoke about action and sacrifice I was reminded of the 1976 Soweto Uprising, when
thousands of students marched in the streets and stood up to
police officers with guns and dogs for their right to inclusive
education. June 16 is celebrated as African Children's Day or
Youth Day across much of the continent to honor the lives

of the young people who took action against the apartheid regime. While there were other protests and killings during that period, it was the images of thousands of young students standing up for their right to learn in their own language in schools that got the world, including the United Nations, to pay closer attention and take action.

By the time the president invited ministers to present their cabinet papers for debate, I was ready. At this moment in history, the lot had fallen to me to take the lead. But I still had a long time to wait. There were more than ten items on the agenda. Over and over again, I heard the president say, "Can someone please move that we adopt the paper by the minister of . . ." In a few instances, he said, "Mr. Minister, would you wish to withdraw this paper?" or "I think this paper needs some more work. . . ." As more and more papers got withdrawn or rejected, I got worried.

Finally, I heard the president say, "I now invite the minister of basic and senior secondary education to present the cabinet paper titled . . ." The paper I would be presenting first was not the one on the ban. That one, in fact, would be the last of three. This was intentional. In consultation with the cabinet secretariat, I chose to first discuss two noncontentious matters. I wanted my colleagues to get used to moving motions to adopt my papers. Of course, there is also a risk to this, because when there are multiple papers by the same ministry, sometimes colleagues can be stricter with the last ones.

The first paper had to do with staffing and it was an easy sell. The second was a proposal to establish what we were calling "LAB schools" across the country. LAB is an acronym for "learn, act, build"; the aim of the schools would be the development and promotion of teaching and learning innovation both within and outside the classroom. Most of the debate centered on the enrollment processes. How could we ensure that all kids who are eligible to attend LAB schools could attend, irrespective of where they lived? What were the selection and exclusion criteria?

All of these questions, I thought, would help foreground the third and most critical paper. So, I took my time and stressed the importance of inclusion, and the accommodations that would be needed to ensure that all could take full advantage. When colleagues insisted on strict minimum grade standards, I pushed back, stressing the need for students from all backgrounds and not just elite urban schools. When the president finally asked if someone would move the motion to support the paper, many hands went up before he finished the sentence.

At this point, my tummy activity increased. I wasn't hungry—so I knew it was my nerves. I thought about asking for a short break to go to the bathroom, but I resisted. I was on a roll and I did not want to disrupt it.

I'm an experienced public speaker. When I was a student, I competed in debates, sat in youth parliament, and played secretary general at a Model United Nations. As an adult, I've addressed schoolchildren and world leaders, spoken at technical conferences to a few interested colleagues, and presented at TED conferences that are streamed to millions. I've curated and hosted global events. I am not just comfortable with public speaking, I'm good at it. But while my goal that day was to "win," that wasn't enough. I needed to strengthen my alliances, and help those who were silent become active. I needed to convince those who were leaning my way to take that last step. As such, the tone of the speech had to be different.

I normally start with a joke. Smiles and laughter break the tension, allowing everyone to focus better on the topic at hand. But when President Bio signaled that it was time for me to present the third paper my throat dried up and all of my jokes slipped out of my head. I took a sip of water and held the mic. Maybe this was not a joking matter, I thought. Eminem's high-pitched voice reverberated in my head: *"You better!"*

"Thank you, Mr. Chairman," I began. "Your Excellency, Honorable Vice President, Chief Minister, colleague Ministers, this paper is about the future of our country. I seek the endorsement of cabinet to authorize me as minister of basic and senior secondary education to reverse the decision of the previous government and lift the ban imposed on pregnant girls from attending school and taking exams."

Chairs moved around. Some people looked away; others reached for their teacups and glasses of water. Several of my colleagues took their pens and started scribbling their points down. I waited for them to settle down. My strategy for the first part was simply to get through the myths and facts as calmly as I could. I knew all the arguments for and against the proposal, so my presentation was tailored toward those who were against it.

"The dimensions, themes, and interests for each of these issues are uniquely different but all centered around fear," I continued. "Fear of the unknown. The fear of 'what if?' and how this would affect the president, the government, and our children."

I took a big breath. Now it was time to present my case.

I had been afraid of the consequences of inaction, whether I could live with myself if I didn't try to change this policy to which I so objected. But what I had finally realized at the state dinner was that my colleagues were just as afraid of the opposite—the consequences of action. They didn't object to the presence of pregnant girls in and of itself; they feared all the bad things they imagined would result from lifting the ban and didn't want to be responsible for them. It would be so much easier just to leave the ban in place.

One of the biggest lessons I learned, a lesson for all activists everywhere, I think, is that you must address people's fears head-on. It always feels safer to do nothing than something, especially when you aren't particularly committed to that something or you oppose it. Lucky for me, I had been in a position of fear many times myself.

During my PhD research, as just one fresh example, I had to deal with this same fear of "what if?" which is really a fear of failure. Fear of failure is perhaps the biggest impediment to leadership, which is largely about taking action. When we act, we put ourselves out there. If we fail, it may cost us our lives, our livelihoods, and our reputation, everything we had worked for up to that point. So, when we are faced with this fear, we don't act. Indecision sets in. That is why we ban things, so we don't have to deal with them. As I worked on my PhD thesis, I used to wonder, what if after all these years and effort, one cannot really create a functional prosthetic socket that's comfortable? One time I went to MIT's chancellor to seek his opinion on a respectable way to quit my PhD program. I was so afraid to fail through action that I was ready to fail through inaction—by giving up.

As I sat there in the cabinet room, I felt like I was defending my PhD all over again. Prior to the defense, Professor Herr reminded me that the real work had already been done; he told me I should lead with a story that would make it clear how significant my invention was and how it could transform the world. My research blended multiple fields—each of which had its own experts—but that day I needed to convince everyone that I was the expert on the intersection of those fields. I remembered the audience listening attentively as I systematically went through the major aspects of my work. I could see my wife in the audience, beaming with pride. Kate was pregnant with Nyaanina at the time, and I felt like I was doing it for my unborn daughter.

Back in the cabinet room, it was the same thing—I was doing this for Nyaanina and Peynina and Kadija. All the months of engagement had come to this. I was afraid, but for this day, I was the expert on the intersection of gender, politics, religion, tradition, negative influence, and child protection, because I had done my research. I was doing it for that pregnant girl with the purple skirt I passed on the road on my first day as minister. I was doing it for my daughters, for their unborn daughters, and for every girl who had been excluded from education. This cabinet defense was the only way.

In one of my freestyle rap songs, I wrote, "I do this for her, do this for the people who can never do this / A radical? Absurd, check the roots." Those girls who are shut out of classrooms because of a government policy could never be in this position to advocate for their own rights. They inspired me to fight through my fear.

"Mr. Chairman, colleague Ministers," I continued, "we are lucky because while there are several myths around this topic, there is also ample evidence surrounding it. I have spoken to fellow ministers, women in the market, parents, students, my children, teachers, religious leaders, and pretty much every voice in society. Please permit me to discuss some of the issues that have been raised and present the evidence for and against those under the themes of politics, religion and morality, and child protection."

I exhaled, felt the weight of my body settle into the chair, and listened to the loud silence.

Not many people want to go against something a president says, certainly not those who owe their positions to him. It is the quickest and surest way to lose one's job in politics. Most people who displease His Excellency do so unknowingly or in rebellion.

I decided to tackle my colleagues' understandable desire for self-preservation first. From the privileged conversations I'd had with the president over the years, it was clear to me that he would rather have an enemy tell him where he was wrong than a friend dress him in borrowed robes. So, I took the bull by the horns.

"Your Excellency," I boldly said. "It may seem like over-turning this ban goes against something you said publicly recently. Yes, that is correct, but that is not the real story." I spoke about how this change could be perceived not as a weakness but as an example of leadership, proving that he listens to the people.

As for the preservation of the government, I argued that the opposition wouldn't be able to use this as a weapon against our party, because all the nation's children would be affected. Everyone in Sierra Leone knew someone who knew someone whose child got pregnant in school. A few more chairs shifted in the room and I could see that some of my colleagues were uncomfortable. I think their discomfort arose from the fact that I was responding directly to some of the things they themselves had said. I avoided direct eye contact with anyone but the president.

I then expanded the scope of the discussion. Sierra Leone, I reminded everyone, plays a leading role in the West Africa subregion. Since the regional court had ruled that the ban was illegal and that the government must overturn it, obeying the court's decision would be a big step toward multilateralism—something the president was a major proponent of. The move could score major political points, not just in Sierra Leone, but across the subregion and the world. The president scribbled something on his papers and the vice president nodded his head in agreement.

Just as I felt I was getting control of the room, I heard one of my colleagues mutter, "Come on, Minister, Sierra Leone is a religious state." I looked up from my notes and without missing a beat said, "I recognize that Sierra Leone can be described as a religious state, Honorable Ministers, and this is why we have engaged religious leaders nationally on this topic. If pregnant girls can sit next to non-pregnant girls in churches and mosques, the houses of God, who are we as mere mortals to prevent that in a school, a house of man?" Since Sierra Leone is a highly tolerant religious nation, I reminded my colleague ministers that we needed to forego imposing any singular interpretation of religious texts. The loudest voices in favor of maintaining the ban, I said, were the handful of religious leaders who happened to have access to not just their pulpit, but a microphone.

The objections then turned toward questions of culture. Change is particularly slow and difficult when it's related to culture and tradition. When proposing an action that goes against the status quo, you will often hear people say things like, "Our culture does not support this." Or, "This is a foreign tradition to us." Or, particularly in the Global South, "We need to keep things that have worked for us as they are, and not be swayed by the West." I had heard all of these objections and more when I had talked with stakeholders. The appeal to tradition and culture is like the famous Hail Mary pass in American football;

it's what people resort to when they don't want to change their position but have exhausted every possible argument.

In fact, the biggest excuse for inaction is almost always some version of "But this is how it's always been. This is our culture; you wouldn't understand." There are many things in culture that do deserve to be preserved, even as our society evolves. But the "this is our culture" argument should never be used to stop debate; there should be nothing in society we can't discuss. And it certainly should never be used to keep hurtful practices in place that consign some members of society to the fringes.

When people play the culture card, the best defense is for someone from that same culture to take a stand and challenge the status quo. Culture is, after all, maintained by the status quo. Consider the debates around female genital cutting. Framing the issue as a binary—a choice between traditional and Western culture—is enough to end the discussion. Any sensitivity to children's rights, informed consent, safe spaces for women, and the like—all of which are reasons to ban this practice, particularly for children—go by the wayside. You are either for tradition and all that comes with it, good and bad, or you are a puppet of foreign governments.

This is also true in far less dramatic circumstances. Families have traditions, like always serving goose at Christmas, that may need to be reexamined when a member of the clan becomes a vegan. Offices do, too. Must bonding exercises always involve a trip to a bar? Could that change if you hired an employee who told you they are in recovery?

I noted to colleagues that various traditions in our society were changing rapidly, as was our culture. We don't notice the changes immediately because they happen so quickly and to almost everyone at the same time. In fact, I realized in that moment, our culture had changed so quickly that a cabinet minister with gold-tinted dreadlocks—that would be me—was making a presentation about a national policy change for girls' education (but I was not going to be the one to point that out). The use of mobile phones had changed our language and our whole way of communicating in less than a decade. It had even changed the way one generation speaks to another. When I call my grandmother on the phone, after "hello" I now add "what's up?"—something that would have been considered disrespectful from a younger to an elder not too long ago. She responds in Mende and we proceed without missing a beat. A few cabinet ministers nodded their heads.

But I wasn't done yet; I had saved my most important argument for last. Before I launched into it, I noticed my palms were sweaty—something I'd never experienced before. Was it real or was Eminem's rap verse running through my head (*"His palms are sweaty, knees weak, arms are heavy"*)? There was no time to find out.

Sierra Leone's Human Rights Commission had supported a study to "identify the factors leading to teenage pregnancy, and the experiences of pregnant teenagers and teenage mothers, particularly in continuing their schooling after birth." The report observed that "in some chiefdoms in Sierra Leone, there continues to be a culture and tradition of arranging marriages between adult men and their nieces." So much for culture and tradition always being things we should support.

Ironically, when opponents of the move to lift the ban on pregnant girls referenced child protection, their remarks were only about protecting non-pregnant girls from pregnant ones. They also suggested that it was in the pregnant child's best interest to remain at home. I argued that the best way to protect the girls—many of whom are definitionally victims of sexual violence because they are under the age of eighteen—is to bring them to school and out of the homes and communities in which they had been violated. I reminded the cabinet that this was in line with the president's vision and governing principles.

Furthermore, school is the safest place for any child, especially girls. We had seen it during the Ebola epidemic, where children in school were far less likely to get infected and where they could receive psychological support as they and their families grappled with the epidemic's effects. At this point the president was visibly nodding his head in agreement and quickly scribbling. This is uncommon during presentations, where he usually holds a blank gaze and jots down things. I saw the surprise on the faces of some of my colleagues.

By the time I finished my presentation, I had carefully addressed all the critical issues and objections I knew opponents to the proposal would have, being sure not to miss one. This was a strategy I learned not from any of the government mentors I've had and not from my professors and not even from Shimon Peres, but from Eminem in the last scene of his autobiographical movie *8 Mile*. In the final freestyle rap battle, his character's strategy is to state all the damning things that his opponent could possibly say about him. He starts from the embarrassing and continues on to the most lurid details of his and his friends' lives, the very airing of which would seem to destroy all of his and their credibility. Only then does he rhyme the strongest punchlines against his opponent that he can muster, all of them based on evidence and data that everyone present knew to be true. As he throws the microphone to his challenger, Papa Doc, he finishes by rapping, "*I don't wanna win, I'm outtie / Here, tell these people something they don't know about me.*"

Boom!

This wasn't exactly *8 Mile*—in fact, it would be hard to think of an environment further removed from it than a cabinet room nearly five thousand miles from Detroit—but by the time I said, "Thank you, Mr. Chairman, I look forward to this cabinet endorsing one of the most transformational policies of our government," I felt like I did on stage in Bo town hall when I was ten. I could see the fear in my opponents' eyes and the support from those who were convinced. For the first time, I sensed that the cabinet might endorse the proposal.

My elation didn't last long. Once the debate began, it became clear that some of my opponents were even more set in their positions. A few people who'd promised their support were not coming through. I didn't take any of it personally; I had learned not to. Cabinet debates are matters that will affect the state and should not be about allegiances but the strength of the data and the arguments. I was fine with dissenting views and didn't think their opinions defined who they were as persons. They needed to champion views and perspectives they had heard and ensure that collectively we were making the right decisions. As it happened, the biggest supporters for the proposal were from unexpected circles. Several cabinet members told me they had also engaged their daughters on the topic. Others shared stories of siblings who had been pregnant in school before the government ban and had gone on to become professionals. They wondered what would have happened to those beloved family members if the ban had been in place. Pro and con, their voices were very emotional.

One of President Bio's superpowers is his ability to keep his emotions in check during debates. He listens closely and gives away as little as possible, even when he is delivering his opinions. Most people talk about not knowing how the president "feels" about them. During the debates, several ministers kept referring to the president's public endorsement of the ban all those months ago, and how a change might be viewed if the cabinet overturned it.

At one point, the president uncharacteristically spoke over a minister, interrupting him to say that no one should worry about what he would say to the public should we decide to overturn the ban. This was the pivotal moment. I saw faces relax and contort; more chairs moved; and ministers stood up to get more coffee and biscuits. The room had been tense; now that the president had addressed the elephant in the room, more people were willing to support my paper. Nearly two hours of passionate discussion later, everyone had spoken at least twice, and I had responded to several rounds of arguments and questions. The president gave his closing remarks and a summary of the debate. At last he said, "Can someone please move . . ."

I don't remember hearing anything after those words or noticing who moved in favor of the motion or who seconded it. But his question would have ended with ". . . that we adopt the paper presented by the minister of basic and senior secondary education to lift the ban on pregnant girls from attending school and to also develop the policy of radical inclusion and comprehensive safety?" All I could feel were the tears streaming down my face. Then I heard "Congratulations, David" from my colleagues, including many who had raised objections at the start of the meeting.

It was for moments like this one that I traded my job in the private sector for an unstable government appointment— and for the opportunity to shape my country's legacy for the better. When I signed up to work with President Bio, it was clear that debate and discussion would exist in our relationship. And I knew he was committed to creating a more just and inclusive society, even if that meant going against what he once believed and publicly stated. Like me, he believes that it is only through action that we can begin to change the world. Sometimes action means doing whatever you can to change other people's minds. Sometimes the action you need to take is to change your own. That's the hardest and bravest one of all.

Still, even in that moment, I knew I had to keep the celebration brief. The work had only just started. I had spent so much time thinking, what if we don't succeed? that I didn't have a plan for, what if we win?

6

Adapting to a New Normal

. . . . .

Discipline and devotion are necessary to the practice of love, all the more so when relationships are just beginning.

—BELL HOOKS

$\mathcal{S}$ome weeks after the cabinet's decision, I visited President Bio and his family at the presidential lodge. Although it was a social visit, the president and I squeezed some serious public sector and governance matters in between our otherwise light chat about his farm, new gadgets, and sports. Before dinner, we relaxed on the teal-green leather couches in his living room as he reminisced about his travels across Sierra Leone as a military officer and, years later, a presidential candidate. He spoke about the nitty-gritty details of certain terrains in the North, the cacao farms in the Southeast, and the mining pits in the East. As his voice became animated, it picked up the beat of the traditional music that was playing on the stereo. I took it all in, making the most of the opportunity to learn about our political party and its history, and about the president himself.

When we sat down for dinner at the long black marble table in the dining room, the topic had switched to potential uses and impacts of drones in Sierra Leone. The food was served buffet style on a sideboard. The president passed me a bowl of salad and poured me some fresh-squeezed orange juice without my asking. We'd spent enough time together by now that we knew what the other enjoyed.

As we ate, our conversation turned to some projects in the education sector. Every few minutes, Amina would come into the room to ask her dad how to pronounce a word in a book she was reading, or to ask me when she could have a playdate with Nyaanina. Just as we were starting dessert, she asked her father to help her with her math homework, which he did in between bites of chocolate ice cream and fruits. As they worked, I looked up at the three large chandeliers with diamond-shaped pendants and wondered what Kate and my kids were talking about at the dinner table at home.

When Amina's homework was finished and the table was cleared, the president poured me some tea and we continued to talk, jumping from tasks to be done over the next few months to his long-term vision for Sierra Leone. As I was getting ready to leave, a serious look crossed his face. After checking to make sure that Amina was out of earshot (she was watching a cartoon in the other room), he took out his phone and asked me to listen to an audio he'd received a few days before.

The second it began, I realized what it was. A popular and revered religious leader in Sierra Leone had delivered a sermon to his followers that contained a stern reprimand for President Bio and me. God was angry with our nation, he said, because of the kind of decisions we were making. One of the worst was overturning the ban on pregnant girls in schools—something that he and his congregation would never accept. How could a God-fearing nation allow pregnant girls in school? What kind of leaders would do something that was so clearly inspired by the devil? We would pay for this, he promised darkly. How? He did not say.

I'd heard all these sentiments before, but I was surprised they were still being expressed after the battle had been fought and won.

Although the president remained outwardly calm, I didn't need an AI emotion recognition algorithm to sense his anger. I told him to turn off the audio, that I'd heard it already. The truth was that I hadn't. A friend had sent it to me and I'd deleted it immediately, but I promised myself now that I'd listen to it fully when I got home. In the same way we listened to our opponents' views before and during our fight for inclusion, I knew we'd have to listen to them after as well if we wanted to ensure that the changes we'd made were going to stick.

President Bio said, "I always say this, change is very difficult. The same people who you try to work for are the ones who will go against you. When we fight against corruption and indiscipline, we have to be very ready, because corruption and indiscipline will fight back. People do not like change, but we have to help them accept change." His words brought back memories of the "new direction" manifesto he'd campaigned on when he ran for president, which had been all about change and perseverance. Seeing my sadness, he smiled and said, *"Paopa Salone Mus Betteh,"* a popular Krio campaign slogan, which translates to "By all means, Sierra Leone will be better."

The president assured me again of his unwavering support for the policy change and urged me not to lose my focus. I thanked him, called goodbye to Amina, and walked outside to my car. During my drive back to the city, I couldn't stop thinking about how much there still was to be done.

There are many challenges that make our daily work difficult at the ministry, including some that plague everyone in government. For example, we periodically have power cuts in the office, which means that the air-conditioning and internet are shut off, bringing productivity to zero while maximally elevating the staff's discomfort. A few days after my visit to the president's lodge, as I sat in the suffocating heat during one of those outages, I received a phone call from my deputy minister Madam Gogra.

During a visit to a school in Freetown, Madam Gogra had inquired about some empty chairs she saw at an examination center. The school leader informed her that the girls were pregnant. Shocked, she asked why they hadn't shown up for the exams. She did not believe the teacher's answer, which was that it was the girls' own choice. The teacher claimed that he had advised the girls to take the exam as per government policy, but explained that they "think pregnancy is the end of their lives."

Madam Gogra knew that teachers tended to blame the girls for their absences from school, when most often it was because the school environment made it nearly impossible for them to attend safely and comfortably. She asked for the girls' addresses and immediately went to their homes.

She found out that one of the girls had been sent to her grandparents' village to deliver her baby. Madam Gogra explained the government's new policy to her parents, about which they were well aware, and urged them to make sure the child returned as soon after delivery as possible to continue her education as a parent learner. It was only then that the parents confessed that they were worried about the kind of support she would receive in school. They also revealed the amount of bullying she had endured from her peers and teachers. I thought back to the concern Gloria had raised in Bombali.

It was yet another reminder that even with the policy change, we still needed to do a lot more than we were to make it permanent. I also realized that while we needed to convince people to accept the new normal, we would never be able to change everyone's mind at once. We certainly wouldn't be able to go to every home or visit every school where a child was barred from class for one reason or the other.

We at the ministry and all of our education stakeholders go out of our way to support pregnant and parent learners. We are constantly thinking of ways to make life easier for them and for any child with special needs. Nationwide, the ministry keeps track of pregnant girls in schools so that it can ensure they are receiving sufficient psychosocial and material support.

Still, exclusion is like cancer. When cancer cells attack the body, they destroy normal cells and keep proliferating until eventually the person dies. Some exclusions, like some cancers, are clearly visible and easy to diagnose. Others can go unrecognized for years. If cancer is caught and treated early, the patient is likely to have a better outcome. But even so, we have to monitor the patient lest they suffer a relapse. That's what we set out to do for pregnant girls in Sierra Leone. And that's what you need to do for any exclusion you identify in your family, community, or nation.

We hadn't solved the problem; we had only caused it to go into temporary remission. We still needed to change hearts and minds. For reference and inspiration, I looked to the ways that different societies had created "new normals" following legislative change.

On April 26, 2000, Vermont became the first state in the US to legalize civil unions and registered partnerships between same-sex couples. Four years later, Massachusetts legalized gay marriage. In 2011, President Obama's administration stopped enforcing the Defense of Marriage Act, a federal law that defined marriage as between one man and one woman. While those policy changes were critical, there was still an immense amount of anti-gay sentiment across America—perhaps even more than there had been before, as social progress often inspires a backlash. It wasn't until June 26, 2015, that the United States of America's Supreme Court voted to make same-sex marriage legal in all fifty states. Whatever happens now, it's undeniable that there has been a sea change in the hearts and minds of Americans on this issue. One thing that contributed to it was television, especially dramas and comedies.

Over the last decade, one TV show in particular helped transform Americans' views on same-sex marriage and gay rights, and that was *Modern Family*—a situation comedy focused on how three modern-day families deal with their children, spouses, and jobs. Through humor and drama, the show, which started in 2009 and ended in 2020, winning over twenty Emmy and Golden Globe Awards along the way, placed thorny issues of inclusion, gender, and same-sex parenting at the heart of popular culture. While it was not the first TV show to have major gay characters or families, it was among the most popular, and it helped normalize the idea of same-sex couples in committed relationships who have children.

Comedy plays two key roles in the establishment of new cultural norms. First, it allows you to feel the pulse of society. The gay characters in *Modern Family* would sometimes joke about themselves as being gay, but in doing so provided an invitation for people to know them better, causing many to question their biases. Second, the fact that the show was a series, and that it was on TV every week, kept the topic of gay rights on everyone's radar. As a student from an African country, I had a unique vantage. Between 2006, when I arrived in Cambridge, Massachusetts, and 2016, when I left, the conversations I had about gay culture with other students, especially those from Africa, evolved from one of curiosity (since we Africans did not talk about this topic in our countries at the time) to acceptance. I'm not saying that *Modern Family* was solely responsible, but I know that in my circle, at least, it contributed.

Now, obviously, jokes can also be used to belittle, to separate and create division. Any child who has spent any time on a playground can tell you that. But just as important, they can be used to advocate for more inclusion. Trevor Noah, the popular host of Comedy Central's *The Daily Show,* does this every day, using the skills he learned as the child of a mother classified as Black and a father classified as white in apartheid South Africa where he grew up. In his book *Born a Crime,* Noah tells how he used humor as a way to belong when he felt excluded: "I learned that even though I didn't belong to one group, I could be a part of any group that was laughing," he wrote. "I'd drop in, pass out the snacks, tell a few jokes." Noah's ability to use comedy as both a cudgel and a way of changing hearts and minds provided a sharp contrast—and in some ways, an antidote—to the Trump presidency, which promoted policies of exclusion (*"Build the Wall"*).

Sierra Leone also uses drama and comedy to normalize culture shifts. *Wan Pot,* a TV series that debuted shortly after the civil war that tore our people apart, brought all of Sierra Leone's tribes and ethnicities together and put them in "one pot." Its producers believed that if citizens saw the Mende,

Temne, Limba, Creole, and Loko people all making fools of themselves, it would bring everyone together. And it did. At 7 p.m. every Saturday, when it aired, the streets of Freetown were quiet, but its homes were filled with laughter. At school, *Wan Pot* jokes were shared as widely as talk about football and the English Premier League.

Perhaps unlike other countries, Sierra Leone inserts comedy into the agendas of its official state functions, where the president and state officials are not just present but sitting ducks. Yes, the US president hosts the White House Correspondents' Association dinner, where he is roasted by a comedian and gets to make jokes himself, but that happens just one day in the year. In Sierra Leone, this happens at least once a week. There's no better way to check the pulse of Sierra Leone's society than to listen to the kinds of jokes comedians tell at these events. If something makes it into one of their comedy skits, then it is on its way to being normalized.

On the matter of pregnant girls attending school, the skits followed an arc. Before the ban was lifted, they featured a dreadlocked Rasta minister who talked about inviting pregnant girls to school. The implication was that the education minister was maybe high on weed (I do not smoke). Then, as our campaign gained steam, they evolved into ridicule of the girls. Once the new policy was in place, the skits were about how cool it is to see everyone in school these days, including pregnant girls and kids with severe disabilities—and this was while there was still plenty of sentiment against the new policy.

When jokes are made today, they are no longer about whether pregnant girls belong in school—that's normal—but they touch quite pointedly, in the manner of Trevor Noah when he's in his crusading mode, on the need to protect girls from rape and other physical violence. Afterward, people talk, think, and ponder their roles in perpetuating these harmful practices, whether by participating in them or remaining silent in the face of them.

Sierra Leone has comedians who spread hate and misogyny as well, but they eventually update their skits as people stop laughing—or make faces and boo them. Whether at the dinner table, at a social gathering, or on a TV show performed in front of the entire nation, the changes in comedy can reflect the changes that are taking place in a society that's moving in the right direction.

As President Bio said, there is nothing easy or certain about change. The religious leader's message to the president and to me made that clear, as did the resistance from many teachers. Comedians could reflect it and nudge it in the right direction. But we still needed more of a plan. As leaders, we needed to create safe places where people could talk about these difficult issues.

For some people, things hardly ever change; for others, change is a constant. Change can happen so slowly that we're scarcely aware that it's happening, and it can take us by surprise. Sometimes we ourselves are part of the transformation or serve as a catalyst for it. But too often, we are left to cope with its consequences on our own.

I fall in the category of those whose lives are marked by constant change, mostly of my own making. As such, I have learned some techniques to navigate the boundaries of change. During my graduate studies at the MIT Media Lab, my mentor Nicholas Negroponte told us that when you are starting a new project, it should take no more than two years to develop a prototype, test, and complete it—and then you should consider doing something else. It is a principle that he himself used at the Lab and one that I have grown to believe as gospel. In fact, I've organized my life into two-year chunks, changing up what I do, where I live, or both.

But after we repealed the ban on pregnant girls, I felt I needed to ignore my two-year rule. If you ever find yourself in government service, you'll soon realize that it takes a lot longer than two years to get anything big done, especially if you want that thing to last. And allowing pregnant girls in schools was just the first step; I wanted to do much, much more. The irony is that my ministerial appointment has no job security; I serve only as long as it pleases His Excellency.

Nonetheless, I knew I needed time to lay the foundations that would make not just this new policy but our whole radical inclusion agenda permanent, or as permanent as anything in civic life can ever be. The lack of job security wouldn't deter me.

In our National Policy on Radical Inclusion in Schools, which was created by all the major education sector stakeholders and ultimately endorsed by the cabinet, we defined radical inclusion as:

The intentional inclusion of persons directly or indirectly excluded (from education) due to actions or inactions. The radical inclusion policy focuses on the removal of all infrastructural, systemic, policy, and practice impediments that limit the learning for any child, as well as creates an enabling and inclusive environment that eradicates stigma, harassment, intolerance, and exclusion for any reason. Radical inclusion is a process and a way of increasing justice and equity in peoples' lives and organizations. The policy particularly emphasizes the inclusion of historically marginalized groups: pregnant girls and parent learners, children with disabilities, children from rural and underserved areas, and children from low-income families. It is about creating an inclusive education system that allows all children in Sierra Leone to thrive.

As policy makers we have a lot of time to think and process change. But new regulations, guidelines, and policies can often come as a shock to the general public, and their initial response is often resistance. Some people will continue to resist, no matter how much you try to deepen their engagement with the issues via comedy and other soft tactics. Not everyone gets with the program. For them, you need a different approach.

We saw the issue of pregnant girls in school as something of a bellwether—if we couldn't guarantee that, then we might as well forget about the rest of our radical inclusion agenda as well. I want to pause here and talk a little bit about the terms I'm using. As I see it, there is a subtle but important distinction between "inclusion" and "equity." Equity is a state, and inclusion is a process to get you toward that state in which everyone enjoys the same opportunity to be present, to participate, to be seen, and to be oneself. Radical inclusion is using all means to ensure constant progress toward that state of equity for all those excluded. Equity is the goal; inclusion is a crucial first step in getting there.

This is where the proverbial rubber hits the proverbial road: every effort to model acceptance you can think of should be employed when you are trying to create a more equitable family, community, or nation—but in the end, you have to be willing to enforce radical inclusion. In a company, for example, you can create codes of ethics for employees and nudge them in the right direction via participation in equity workshops, but if someone adamantly refuses to go along, you might have to end their employment, even if they are among your best-performing staff. If you tolerate recalcitrance, it gives the impression that you are engaging in nothing more than window dressing.

History tells us that at various times, institutional power and even force may be needed to protect a change in policy and ensure that everyone knows you are serious about moving forward on the path to equity. In 1954, when the US Supreme Court ruled unanimously in *Brown v. Board of Education of Topeka* that racial segregation in public schools is unconstitutional, many local governments and school administrations still refused to allow Black people to enroll in all-white schools. Images of Black students being escorted into schools by military and police officers, running gauntlets of vicious, violent, racist attacks by local citizens, were seen all over the United States and the world. The National Guard was an essential tool in enforcing desegregation. If force had not been used, the change in laws would have been for naught. Even with it, the further introduction of affirmative action, something that is still under attack, was a necessary step to ensure that those who were previously excluded could fully benefit from the policy change.

Luckily, we did not need the military or police to escort pregnant girls to school. But we did need to deploy tools for change management that ranged from effective public communication and home visits, like Madam Gogra's, to wholesale system reengineering. I also employed some techniques I learned in the academic and private sectors.

Barely two months after I received my PhD in biomechatronics from the MIT Media Lab, Kate, Nyaanina, and I packed our bags and flew to Kenya. The first time Kate and I went to Nairobi, we had done so as a honeymoon gift to ourselves. This time, I had been hired as a data scientist at IBM Research Africa. When I announced my plan to change careers after completing my PhD, my family summoned me to a meeting. "But what about the prosthetic work, who will continue it?" they asked. "Why are you doing this now, after all the time and energy you put into your thesis?"

My mom was among the hardest to convince that what I was doing made sense.

Here's what I told her: ever since I left Sierra Leone, I'd had a clear vision—to do high-impact work with direct benefits for my country, and ultimately to return. The primary project I would be assigned to at IBM involved the deployment of a system in Port Loko that analyzed multiple quantitative and qualitative health data to support decision-making in disease surveillance. It had been built in response to the

Ebola emergency of 2014, so my new work was all of a piece: its goal was still to help the people of my homeland.

While that project eventually won international recognition and awards, an equally important project took place in Tanzania. Working on it taught me a lot about the unique power and influence of those who sit on the inclusion-exclusion boundary, and the crucial role they can play in promoting radical inclusion. Let me tell you a bit about this project before I explain exactly what I mean by the "inclusion-exclusion boundary."

In 2017, I took a team of researchers to Tanzania to collect a large labeled dataset of images of Africans (men, women, young, old) expressing various emotions. These would then be used by IBM researchers across the world to develop better machine-learning algorithms for image and emotion recognition. I'd been inspired by Joy Buolamwini, my former colleague at the MIT Media Lab, who in several academic papers had clearly identified the exclusion of Black and especially Black female faces in machine-learning data sets used to train AI algorithms. The impact of the exclusion was real and significant.

I had experienced it for myself when I was at the Media Lab. The biomechatronics group shared floor space with another research group called "affective computing," which developed algorithms that could identify people's emotions based on their facial expressions. It was always a bit unsettling for me when their prototypes either failed to recognize me at all or were unable to correctly classify my smile as a smile—even though it recognized white colleagues who had been scanned a similar number of times. It wasn't just me the algorithms failed; it was anyone who looked like me. That was why I reached out to researchers, including Joy, and mobilized resources within IBM to set up a "Smile for Science" exhibition booth at the TEDGlobal conference in Arusha.

I had not foreseen the depth and impact of the project at the time we were first developing it. What brought it home to me was the reaction of a young female Kenyan IBM scientist on my team. Purity—who is currently pursuing her postgraduate education in computer science in the United States—approached me on the last day of the conference to tell me that her experience at the booth had changed her life. It made her realize, she said, that as an IBM employee writing the algorithms, she was one of those excluding, at the same time that, as a Black female user, she was being excluded. Sadness and disappointment do not fully capture Purity's emotions as she expressed how hard it was to accept that our solutions did not "see" smiles of joy in the people who looked like us. The sad irony was that the computer was equally oblivious to the emotions of anger, frustration, and sadness in our Black faces.

It was during this exchange that I came to see the role of

those sitting on the inclusion-exclusion boundary of change, people like Purity and me who were, in that instance, both excluder and excluded. I had thought the boundary was a bright line. My work at IBM helped me understand that it's more like a border region between two nations that is constantly being redrawn, with people now on one side, now on the other, sometimes in both simultaneously and sometimes in a no-man's-land.

For example: How does a mixed-race family like mine engage during conversations about Black Lives Matter? Do the ways we express our opinions depend in some part on the context and who else is in the room? The simplest thing to do when on the border is to code-switch or stay silent, especially if you don't always have the energy to engage in the emotional labor of breaking down exclusion barriers. How am I preparing my own mixed-race children for life on the inclusion-exclusion border? My daughter Nyaanina, who was also at the TEDGlobal conference in Arusha, visited the booth several times. While it was fun for her to watch the funny or scary videos on screen that were designed to elicit emotions, I felt sad that her feelings weren't being accurately captured by the algorithms her father's company was using.

Then something else occurred to me.

While sitting on the inclusion-exclusion border can be painful, it is at that very border that we find some of the greatest opportunities for transformational impact. Whenever you are both included and excluded, you are being given a unique and beautiful opportunity to help fight for and normalize a new state of greater inclusion, where the newly included and previously excluding can thrive. This is possible because you are "in" with both sides, if not always equally so. Earlier in the book, we saw how trusted voices are needed to build a co-alition for change. They are needed even more once barriers are broken.

Within IBM, they listened to me in a different way than they listened to Joy, who was seen as an outsider judging our solutions. Purity and I used our in-between status to help bridge the gap between how our colleagues at IBM Research developed data and how our fellow Africans at TED could contribute as full participants in the creation of future algorithms that would "see" them better. I needed similar bridges to make the cabinet decision allowing pregnant girls to attend school stick.

So I set out to find advocates who lived on the border of exclusion and inclusion. It didn't take me long to realize who those people are: teachers and administrators, both those who had always been on the side of access for pregnant girls and those who started off opposed to it but then switched to our side.

That is why I gave more voice to Gloria and teachers like

her, so they could help us navigate our challenges with school administrators who were refusing admission to pregnant girls. I believed those holdouts lacked the tools—the language even—they needed to accept those they had previously marginalized. So, we invited pregnant girls who had returned to school and passed their exams to come to meetings and speak up. We also invited their classmates to reflect on their experiences. Teachers who believed in our mission organized the events and led the discussions.

You can't simply change policy and ask staff to implement it; you have to show them how by holding their hands and giving them the tools they need to implement it. Within my team, Dr. Yatta Kanu, the chief education officer, became the biggest advocate of radical inclusion. With staff, colleagues, or anyone else who was willing to listen, she would drive the need to follow the detailed Radical Inclusion Implementation Plan she had developed. Her approach was blunt but effective: *follow the manual.*

Ultimately, you need a large number of enthusiastic and vocal influencers to drive change. Silence or muted engagement is not enough. In our case, we needed teachers and community leaders who were truly convinced about the necessity for change to be bridges to those who were still holding out. We needed to institutionalize the change by developing organizations to work at the community and grassroots level until things became normal. All this can take a long time, but you have to start somewhere.

My friend Asmaa James from *Good Morning Salone* knew too many pregnant girls; after she came around to our side she developed a convert's enthusiasm for radical inclusion. Once the ban was lifted, she established an organization called Girls Plus. As I mentioned, the ministry was already keeping track of the number of pregnant girls in schools, particularly those taking exams, through its annual school census. But there was no system in place that could follow up with individual girls during the school year, asking them what kind of support they needed and providing it. To fill that gap, Girls Plus vowed to reach out to pregnant girls in every district. The organization engaged either in person or via telephone with all the registered pregnant girls twice a week. It also supported local stakeholders.

One day, Asmaa made an appointment to see me at my office. At a school in an outlying district she'd visited, she told me, a comfortable sitting area had been built where parent learners could breastfeed their babies during lunch periods. She took out her phone to show me an image of a parent learner breastfeeding her child (the teenager's face was blurred; Asmaa takes the privacy of her beneficiaries very seriously). Another photo showed a schoolteacher holding a baby while the mother completed her classwork. The principal of the school was among those helping in various ways. While many schools do not have such support systems, everywhere Asmaa and her team went, pregnant girls and parent learners were being taken care of.

So that was the good news; we were making progress. But Asmaa quickly reminded me of something that I knew all too well: that sometimes the excluders weren't simply people who were not in favor of change, but people who had benefited profoundly from the status quo—a status quo that often protected people who'd done terrible things.

As an activist, Asmaa wanted to pursue justice whenever a pregnancy was a product of rape. But this was extremely challenging. In the laws of Sierra Leone, sexual intercourse of any kind with a child who is not yet eighteen is punishable by a minimum of fifteen years in prison and a maximum of life imprisonment. When Asmaa disclosed her intention to seek justice, often the victims and their parents would refuse to identify the father or indeed talk to her at all. In some instances, the girls would stop coming to school. While justice is important to Asmaa, the primary goal of Girls Plus is to get girls back in school, so she learned to keep her conversations about justice for the girls separate from her outreach.

Asma knew that some of the men who had raped the girls were the very same men who provided for them and their families, including community elders and businessmen.

Sometimes teenagers traded sex for rides to school on the back of transport motorbikes. When she told me that, I made a note to follow up with the motorbike riders' union.

In Sierra Leone, 21 percent of fifteen-to-nineteen-year-old girls have begun childbearing. Many suffer complications, both physical and psychological. Asmaa's organization was committed to following up with the new mothers for a period of three months after birth (the length of a school term), after which they would be strongly encouraged to re-enroll. In addition to the high mortality rates associated with teenage pregnancies (40 percent of maternal deaths in Sierra Leone are of pregnant women and girls below age nineteen), post-partum health issues, including obstetric fistulas, are major issues. For young girls already facing social challenges and marginalization, such health issues can easily become too much of a weight to carry. Postpartum care and services were crucial for supporting the policy. The problem, however, is too immense: Asmaa confided in me that Girls Plus was already overwhelmed.

That was a cruel realization. We had changed the law. We were trying to change attitudes. But unless we could change the lives of those girls and vastly increase the support available to them, a large share of a generation of girls would still be left behind.

"The kids really want to continue their education, Mr. Minister. But you have to help them, particularly those who have delivered," Asmaa said. When Grace came to the door to let me know that my next appointment was waiting, I asked for more time.

Sierra Leone doesn't just have a high maternal mortality rate; it has a high infant mortality rate. It's all connected, of course. When the parents of teenage mothers abandon the girls, the girls have to cope on their own. Asmaa suggested that I speak with other organizations to learn what else could be done.

Community engagement, government commitment, and philanthropies all have roles to play in creating and sustaining systemic change. Without them, this change we were so proud of might be doomed.

When Asmaa left, I felt dispirited. But then I remembered that there was one group I had not thought about nearly enough, and I felt some hope. You might be able to guess what it was.

In July 2021, I visited a number of schools and communities around the Western Area Urban and Rural Districts accompanied by members of my team and some visitors from abroad. At one of our stops, we gathered with members of a Boys and Girls Club under a tree. One of the girls turned on a solar-powered radio and we listened to an episode of a program about menstrual hygiene. The program featured lively music, and the students moved their heads and bodies to its beat. Afterward, we asked the students how they felt about the inclusion of pregnant girls in schools.

The girl who had turned on the radio spoke first; she said that at first she had felt it was a bad idea, for all the reasons that we usually heard. Then she added something intriguing. "When a girl becomes pregnant," she said, "she stops being a girl and becomes a woman, and I do not want to be coming to school with women. This is what I used to think. Today, I now know that they themselves are still girls, and are victims, and we should support them. When I see pregnant girls in schools, I feel sorry for them. It makes me not actually want to get pregnant while in school."

Just as we were wrapping up, one of the boys raised his hand. He was about twelve years old and wanted to share what he had learned from the club. Before he joined it, he said, he had not known anything about girls' cycles. Now, he understood that everyone needed to support the girls. If a girl was having cramps, boys should bring her water. If boys and girls share the same bathrooms, then boys should make certain that the girls have all the time in them that they need. This student had a fundamental understanding of the challenges that girls face in school, and it was clearly normal for him, unlike most other males in our society, to talk frankly about even their periods and what he could do to make their lives better and safer. The other boys appeared to share his sentiments, which made me smile from ear to ear. Here were young people being radically inclusive.

Beyond Illusion

7

Beyond Inclusion

. . . . .

Be observant, unassuming, and pragmatic. All others
will fall in line.

—DR. JAMES C. BOIMA

The kind of systemic changes that radical inclusion demands can only come from sustained and definitive actions
at both the micro and macro, or individual and societal, levels. Once those actions are taken, they must be continuously
backed up and protected by every stakeholder. It's one thing
for the majority of people to accept a new normal; it's quite
another to make certain the hard-won gains aren't eroded
over time. Without vigilance and constant effort, you can—
through the efforts of bad actors or simply through your own

complacency and lack of commitment—wind up exactly where you started, or in a place that's even worse. The key is to be perpetually mindful of everything that's going on around you.

Allow me to illustrate this with an example from my college days. In 2007, less than one year into my Harvard undergraduate experience, a group of friends—all of them Black students from the Harvard African Students Association, Association of Black Harvard Women, and the Harvard Black Men's Forum—were participating in an afternoon of fun and games in the Harvard quad when an unfortunate incident occurred. Sangu Delle, a student from Ghana and one of my close friends, had invited me to come as well. I don't remember why I couldn't attend, but I remember feeling traumatized when I learned what happened. Someone had called the Harvard University Police Department and reported that people who were not Harvard students were trespassing. I imagine the caller specified that these supposed non-Harvard students were Black; at any rate, the police responded in force, and demanded that the students—who were merely playing Frisbee—present their student IDs.

The indignity of having to prove their right to use a community space that they had every right to be in didn't just leave them with a sense of exclusion; it was humiliating for all Black Harvard students. As word of the incident spread on listservs, Black students held protests in Harvard Yard, holding signs that read I AM HARVARD and calling for an end to racial profiling. This led to meetings and discussions between students and the administration and promises of institutional changes. We were skeptical, but we decided to end the protests. Even so, the incident shaped the way that many of us Black and African students felt on the Harvard campus for the rest of our time at the school.

Sometime in 2018, eight years after we both graduated, I saw that Sangu was posting stories on social media about similar incidents that were still happening at Harvard. He shared news articles from *The Harvard Crimson,* the campus newspaper, reporting that the university police were still profiling Black students, singling them out for treatment that was very different from what other students received.

Sure, progress has been made. But the key question is if it has been maintained, or whether in some respects things are being allowed to revert to where they were before. Well before we enrolled at Harvard, Black alumni shared experiences that were similar to what happened in 2007 and sadly, what is still happening more than a decade later.

When I moved to the MIT Media Lab after graduating from Harvard in 2010, there were as many men named David across all the different labs as there were women among the newly admitted students. David was a popular name for my generation—the fourth most common, in fact—but I mention this to illustrate how few women there were in the lab, less than 10 percent. In the biomechatronics group alone, there were two Davids. I was one of those Davids and another was David Hill, who is also Black. Gender wasn't the only thing the Media Lab needed improvements in—there was only a handful of Black students in the lab. Both of us had several unpleasant experiences on campus.

David Hill was once followed closely by MIT police as he walked along the famous "infinite corridor" from Massachusetts Avenue to the entrance of the Media Lab, where they stopped and questioned him because they claimed he fit the profile of someone they were looking for, a Black man, who, they said, was also wearing khakis and a hoodie. He arrived at the lab feeling at his lowest. How was he expected to show up and contribute to research the same way as other students if he had to go through such indignities? I was sad for him, but all I could do was tell him I was sorry and give him the space to grieve.

There was a custodian at the lab named Cornell. Cornell was a much older gentleman with gray hair, who wore glasses and always had a charming smile on his face. The only similarity between Cornell and me was that we both had dreadlocks. Well, we're also both Black and from regions colonized by the British (Cornell is from the Caribbean). On numerous occasions, fellow students and other staff called me Cornell. One time, I was in the middle of an intense Ping-Pong game on the second floor when a student interrupted me as I was about to return a smash to ask me to set up a table on the fifth floor. Distracted, I missed the shot. "I am not Cornell," I said firmly.

I doubt she understood the impact that her mistake had on my experience at the Media Lab, but it was part of a pattern. David and I were on a committee set up by the Lab to address inequality in the institution, which included students, faculty, and staff. One evening, right after a meeting of the committee, I was walking behind a white colleague as he entered a building. It was cold out, and I didn't want to take off my gloves and find my ID card, so I slipped in behind him. To my astonishment, he turned around and stopped me, demanding to see my ID. When I told David, all he could say was, "Sorry, man."

While frustrating, simply being at the Lab at all was a beginning; in time, hopefully, there will be many more Blacks there as well, normalizing the inclusion. Harvard and MIT are making progress, but are they doing enough to safeguard and build on it?

Campuses like Harvard and MIT, which for decades or even centuries were exclusively male and almost entirely white, are becoming increasingly focused on inclusion, and not just of race, but gender, sexuality, disability, and more, and rightly so. But so much more still needs to be done and for this to happen—more protests, more discussions, more committee meetings, and more people dropping to a knee during the national anthem. Those leading the fight must be openly supported by the administrations and not negotiated with in silence.

Just as important as consolidating and building on gains is another allied issue: Are our institutions doing enough to extend their commitment to inclusion and equity so that it includes *every* group that has been pushed to the margin and kept there?

At the Lab, David and I worked to change institutional mindsets about race. But we also wanted to improve the lives of people with physical disabilities. In fact, that is why we had both come to MIT. But outside of our research, we felt there was little enthusiasm and commitment for expanding and protecting the rights of the disabled.

The struggle for equal rights for the disabled is a crucial example of the need for change, how difficult it can be to make change, and how hard it is to make change stick. It was only in 1990 that the United States instituted a law prohibiting discrimination against people with disabilities, and there are still huge barriers to full inclusion. A Sierra Leonean cousin of mine in Texas has a son named after me who is on the autism spectrum. Having a child who is Black and has a special need means that my cousin and his wife have it doubly hard when it comes to ensuring that he can get the care and education that are available to other children. At many points, they have had to provide care and educational experiences for Moinina at home because of the challenges they experienced in the public system.

When I look back on the work I've done in this area, I'm proud to have contributed something, but I know there is still a long way to go. My PhD adviser Hugh Herr and I regularly exchange ideas about ways to improve conditions for amputees. A major part of me still feels connected to my research; I often engage students with disabilities during my school tours. In fact, I keep a 3-D printer in my office at the ministry and periodically draw new socket designs at my desk.

In mid-2021, I received a text message from Hugh asking that I call him back immediately. I did and he shared an idea for how we could finally implement a concept we had developed over a decade earlier. He was going to establish a center for bionics at MIT that would be able to design and manufacture prosthetics remotely. This distributed model has the promise to bring justice through inclusion to every patient who has lost a limb.

As great as this sounds, my optimism is tempered, because this new proposal uses some of the same language you see in our proposals from ten years ago. Hugh and his team are pushing through with their plans, and so far about a dozen patients have been fitted in Sierra Leone with prosthetics through the program. Another partnership is focused on training quality prosthetists locally. But outside of academia, disability and inclusion issues are under-resourced and are often not a priority for governments and large corporations. This isn't a criticism of the brilliant people who have led the charge on this issue; it's an example of how hard it is to make change permanent and to keep moving forward in a world that is at best often uninterested, if not outwardly hostile.

Throughout history, we see people whose work, advocacy, and lives inspire us to reimagine our fight for inclusion. Consider the Mexican artist Frida Kahlo, who not only had an immense influence on artists but on activists from all over the world—feminists, members of the LGBT+ community, racial minorities, and people with disabilities. Through the power of her self-portraits in particular she brought attention to the complexities of how we think and feel about healthcare, pain, politics, beauty, and death. As is so often the case with groundbreaking geniuses like Kahlo, the attention that is paid to her after her death far exceeds what she received during her lifetime.

My South African friend and mentee Eddie Ndopu was diagnosed with spinal muscular atrophy at age two and wasn't expected to survive past age five. Today he has an Oxford degree and advocates for inclusion of people with disabilities at the UN, the World Economic Forum, and on pretty much every other important global platform. Eddie and I met when he was in high school; he is over thirty now and dreams of being the first person with an acute disability to go to space. Eddie is also a champion for LGBT+ communities.

I know that access to school for pregnant girls in Sierra Leone is something that we can't yet take for granted, that we need to continue our efforts to normalize it while remaining ever vigilant. I also know that we need to do much more. But these days I am spending most of my energy and political capital to make sure we don't go backward.

In December 2020, the archbishop of the Roman Catholic diocese of Makeni invited me to be a keynote speaker at the St. Francis Secondary School Prize Giving and Speech Day activities. There are over twelve thousand schools in Sierra Leone that I superintend, and hundreds ask me to participate in such events. While I review every invitation, my default is to delegate them to someone else on the leadership team, because I could give such speeches every day and would have no time for any other work.

This invitation, however, was different, and not just because the bishop delivered it personally. St. Francis alumni comprise the elite political class for both parties, many of whom can be relied on to show up at the school's events. So, it's something of a melting pot when it comes to politics. If my goal was to consolidate gains and elevate inclusion as a national topic on the agenda of both major parties, then I had to give the invitation proper consideration. Even before I responded, my colleague Timothy Kabba, the minister for mines and mineral resources, gave me a call and told me that I had to say yes. As the youngest members of the cabinet, Tim and I often support each other in and out of the cabinet room. He was elated when I agreed to attend, as we could use the occasion to show "them" (the political opposition) what we are made of.

Tim was right: it seemed like everyone with political interests in the northern region showed up at Makeni that weekend. At the high table with me were several members of the past APC government, the current opposition. Immediately to my left, in fact, was Dr. Samura Kamara, the APC's leader. Dr. Kamara talked extensively with me about his work, his history, and his vision for Sierra Leone. It was not the first time we met, but this time it felt almost like he was campaigning just for me. I listened. He said that he was a great admirer of our work at the ministry of education, that he followed all our programs on the radio, and he asked to schedule a meeting with me when we returned to Freetown.

I wasn't the only representative of the current government at the high table. To my right was the minister of technical and higher education, and next to him was the Honorable Alpha Timbo, my immediate predecessor in my role, who was currently the minister of labor and social security. In the tense and polarized political climate of Sierra Leone, having members of the current government and the opposition come together to talk across party lines was good for the country and it was good for the cameras, too. The entire event was being streamed live. It was, I thought, a golden opportunity for us to model the spirit of democracy. Then it became something quite different.

In between the chitchat with former and current ministers, I listened to some of the speakers, and I did not like what I was hearing. There were numerous requests for more government support and timelier provisions of subsidies. There were complaints about teachers' salaries and other granular issues like the unavailability of textbooks. These are all valid issues, but such school events should celebrate the students' skills and excellence. The content and the tone of the speeches were increasingly political.

Of course, free speech is a crucial component of democracy, and I appreciated the opinions being expressed, even if I suspected that the speeches were coordinated. But now that the event had taken a political turn, I would need to chuck the speech I had been intending to give and deliver a different set of comments, because a national audience was watching.

I put my written speech back in its folder, opened my notebook, and began to draft some new talking points. Precisely because the audience of nearly one thousand was all boys (it's a boys' school) plus only a few women who were there as guests or were alumni of a nearby female school, I decided to speak about radical inclusion and the importance of community engagement at all levels for the success of education at a national level.

When it was my turn at the dais, I immediately confronted the elephant in the room: the gender privilege of being boys and men in our society. It begins in the home, I said, where the chores that boys are expected to do require less time commitments than girls' and the men routinely eat the tastiest and most nutritious part of their meals, leaving the lesser cuts of meat for the women and children. I urged the audience to do everything in their power to protect our girls, and I spoke about the ways in which we could all support the new policies of the government, including radical inclusion and comprehensive safety, a policy geared at making school the safest space for a child—physically, psychologically, and emotionally.

As I continued, I could hear the movement of the leaves

on the trees in the quadrangle at the heart of the school; the audience was *that* silent. However, I was speaking not just to those in the quadrangle but to everyone who was glued to their TVs and Facebook Live. I challenged the alumni to support and pay for the services of all the volunteer teachers, and invited the teachers to think about their jobs as far more than employment but as an act of service. My father had been a teacher at St. Francis in the 1970s and he had many fond memories of the school and the profession. As I shared his story, I invited the parents and community stakeholders to become agents of change, and to monitor and solidify the changes we had made.

Then I took a breath. The most important part of my speech was next. I didn't know how it would be received.

I also had extended family who were alumni of the school, I said. There was nothing surprising or controversial about that, of course. But how was it, I wondered aloud to everyone listening, that we were still addressing the same banal and basic challenges that my relatives had told me they experienced as students over the course of decades? For example, how was it that we were still permitting bullying and open displays of sexism, and tolerating language that was disrespectful or worse to half of our population?

I challenged everyone listening, myself included, to be the agents of the change we want to see in our homes, our schools, our societies, and our country. When I finished, it took a second for the audience to realize I was done. "Thank you for your attention," I said. Then, as I turned to walk back to my seat, the quadrangle erupted in applause. I hadn't been invited to give a political speech but by the way those seated to my right applauded and from the faces of those on my left, the opposition, who were also smiling, even if they weren't applauding, I knew I'd hit the spot.

My speech was political but not partisan; there was nothing I said that couldn't be embraced by people from all parties. I should add, too, that I mention the applause not to let you know how good my speech was (though I do admit I think it was pretty good), but because it demonstrates that there was a hunger for this kind of message. Across the board, the younger generation craves leadership that is inclusive and forward-looking. We want leaders who are accessible, who understand our history and are driven to heal our differences. That is what attracted me to politics.

Immediately after I sat down, Minister Timbo, my predecessor, leaned in and said, "This radical inclusion thing, I don't know how you did it, but when I was minister of basic education, I was almost fired the first time I issued a press release saying that pregnant girls could return back to school." We both laughed awkwardly. He went on to tell me how various senior members of government demanded that he retract the press release that countered the ban. The fact that he was almost fired for doing what I had done made me think about how narrow our path to change had been, and how much could have gone awry along the way. It also deepened my commitment to getting society to continue to understand and embrace the importance of inclusion, and to widen the circle so it could include many others.

Nothing becomes ingrained in culture and society without the support of civil society organizations like churches, unions, other collective bargaining groups, and other nongovernmental organizations. I have a love-hate relationship with the civil society organizations in Sierra Leone. When they work well, they are great and essential for permanent transformation in all sectors. Consider, for example, the marches for peace during the civil war in the 1990s; the national fight to beat Ebola between 2014 and 2016; and the upholding of democratic principles—none of those things would have succeeded without their engagement.

But civil society organizations are only as good as their leaders. When they are led by greedy, vindictive, selfish, and attention-grabbing individuals, they are a thorn in the side of the government and can do a lot of harm. Still, no matter who the leaders are or what other motives those organizations might have, without them, permanent change cannot occur.

This is true everywhere. Think of the role these organizations play in any community and you soon realize their immense power, usually (but not always) as a force for good. Think of the volunteer committees and community action groups in your workplace or neighborhood. Think of the way the children in your family will often band together to raise the consciousness of the adults. In most cases, these people are devoting their time and energy to make their world—our world—a slightly better place. So, my message to anyone trying to make and solidify change is to involve these groups, recognize that they are run by humans who are by nature complex—but whenever possible, give them the benefit of the doubt.

Also, remember that the path to justice will mean stepping away from the status quo, which isn't always pleasant or easy for those that reside comfortably within it.

I see regular protests outside my office window from the disability community in Sierra Leone. This is not because the leaders of these groups believe we are not trying our best, but because they know that without their constant engagement and demands, it is easy for those who aren't in their community to forget their issues or, if they do remember, to give them low priority. They know that many people wouldn't even notice if the slender gains they have made were to disappear.

Soon after I gave the speech at St. Francis, the president

pledged the provision of buses for five special needs institutions across the country (mostly schools for the blind and deaf). When they were delivered about a year later, a leader within the Sierra Leone Union of Disabled Individuals publicly attacked me for being biased and advocating only for certain "privileged" and "visible" disability groups. At first, I was taken aback, but then realized that he was doing exactly what he was meant to—advocating for those who are left out, pushing relentlessly for systemic change until no one is excluded.

There were, however, other organizations with very different agendas. I granted them the benefit of the doubt for as long as I could, but eventually had to speak out.

Some of the social service organizations loudly questioned my credibility because of the speed with which the ban had been overturned. Unlike Minister Timbo, who noted the speed of change and inquired about how this was achieved, those organizations suggested that I must have done something shady to get the results I did. Several had been in support of the ban publicly and were still fighting against the new government policy. Some insisted that there wasn't enough data or sufficient consultation behind our decision, and that we had not done enough to encourage stakeholder engagement after the process. As public criticism grew and more and more lies were told, I had to act.

Since we knew the negative sentiments were not universal and did not cut across all civil society organizations, I took to the radio again. On every talk show, I called out organizations on things they had said that were not true and acknowledged their positions that were correct. I pointed out which of the organizations had come to me to lobby for specific projects and financial support and had been refused as part of my duty to manage our public resources efficiently and fairly. I explained how they got angry, and how several decided to oppose me on everything I did, putting their own pecuniary interests ahead of the work of the ministry. I remembered President Bio's words: corruption will fight back, and indiscipline will fight back. I was experiencing this firsthand.

That said, my goal was maximum transparency; I tried to address every issue I could. While the groups who advocated positions that I needed to challenge were in the minority, they were exceedingly vocal, thanks to radio and social media. And while some of them were compromised, others were good organizations that were simply on the wrong side of history on one issue.

Many other excellent civil society organizations reached out to help. Engaging them directly in our efforts was critical, because they are an essential link between the government and the citizens. They have the local networks and, most important, a mandate to discuss issues and policies with the public.

They also reflect citizens' concerns back to the government. For the population to widely accept this new policy change, we would need to have as many of these organizations on our side as possible, but it was proving tough.

The major challenge was that some of the opposing organizations had spent years supporting the ban. So, even though popular opinion had changed, they believed that if they supported this new position, it would erode trust with their constituencies. If they were wrong about this issue, what else could they be wrong about? The leader of one organization confronted me immediately after the policy change, demanding to know what had changed in the data within a few months of my appointment to warrant such a massive change. Sensing that his main concern was about being right or wrong, I assured him we were giving full consideration to new government policies no matter what our previously held beliefs might be. "Nothing changed with the data and the evidence," I said. "We just analyzed, understood, and were able to present it differently." I don't mean to imply that we cherry-picked data to support our position. In fact, it was quite the opposite. We took a broader view of the data and considered it within a larger context.

For example, we focused not just on the issue of pregnant girls in school, but on girls' general welfare and education. For starters, we wanted to understand why teenage pregnancy rates were so high. We learned that dozens of schoolgirls got pregnant around the time of their examinations. Many chiefdoms do not have examination centers, so children taking any of the three national transition exams were often forced to travel to a larger chiefdom or a district headquarter town. Some spend several weeks in a completely new environment, with no parental guidance, often sharing rooms with other students. As a result, they are extremely vulnerable to sexual exploitation. To mitigate this risk for younger students, we provided all chiefdoms with examination centers. The government also provided adult literacy centers in all chiefdoms and accelerated learning centers to support parent learners who have been out of school.

The data had shown that the policy change would do nothing to decrease the number of girls getting pregnant— that was undeniably true. But taking the wider view, it was clear that there were other actions we could take that would decrease the number of girls who became pregnant. And the data certainly didn't justify punishing girls who had been raped by denying them a future.

Our engagements with civil society organizations paid dividends. Today, nearly all of the organizations that opposed the change now support it. As it happened, the tide of public opinion had already been turning and just needed a bit more time. As the public changed its views, the organizations decided they wanted to be in the "cool" club and embraced radical inclusion.

To drive change within any organization, you need to add resources and engage in dialogue—up to a point. But there should also be social and financial costs for people and entities who choose to oppose moves toward greater inclusion. In the same way that we don't sit down and drink beer with white supremacists, we shouldn't socialize with or provide financial support to people who actively exclude others, whether they are leaders of civil society organizations or colleagues at the office.

I know this is tough. But to be clear, I'm not talking about isolating or punishing people who carelessly or unknowingly use an offensive term, or who are clearly good at heart but have a way to go on their journey, which is pretty much all of us. I'm talking about people who exhibit behavior that is designed to exclude others and who do so knowingly, even profiting financially from their prejudices. If we want to create an environment that is conducive to change, we have to address such behavior immediately and without equivocation.

I religiously follow soccer, tennis, golf, and Formula One motor racing. Since I was a child, all of these sports have received their fair share of criticism because of their lack of inclusiveness. Athletes need to address this. Throughout her career, Serena Williams called out the racism and sexism of many umpires; Lewis Hamilton, who is not just the first Black driver to win a race but the only Black driver currently on the circuit, took a knee with other drivers at Formula One races following Colin Kaepernick's protests against racist policing in the United States and in support of the Black Lives Matter movement. England's soccer players at the 2021 European Championships did the same, to the applause of their fans. All of these actions are efforts to raise awareness of the systemic and structural policies and practices of exclusion that have lasted for centuries. While there can be no corrective cabinet decisions at the global level, individual actions like these all help to accelerate and solidify social progress.

It's clear what the governing bodies of these sports need to do to make their sports less racist and more inclusive, and to safeguard the lives and mental health of their athletes. It's also clear that they often fail to do it, or only do so after immense public pressure is brought to bear. But it's easy to criticize those sports officials and others in the public eye. We also need to apply the same standards to ourselves and our own communities.

We need to ask ourselves whether the spaces where we live, work, and socialize are safe and inclusive; whether we tolerate behavior that we shouldn't and what effect this has; and whether we give enough of our support to legitimate protests when they occur. Radical inclusion demands no less.

But, as I have come to realize, none of us can do this alone, nor can it be on a onetime basis; we need to recognize that it's much easier for people to default to the status quo. In the absence of constant vigilance, baser instincts often do win the day.

As it happened, the England team I just mentioned made it to the finals of the European Championships in 2021, where they played against Italy. It was a hard-fought match and they lost on penalty kicks in the end. The players who missed their shots were all young and Black. All of them were deluged with hate and racist abuse, online and chanted from the stands, both abroad and in their home communities.

Officialdom had to act. Prime Minister Boris Johnson and several global leaders condemned the hate speech. And the English Football Association issued a statement that spoke to the need for more action by the government and social media companies.

"We will do all we can to support the players affected while urging the toughest punishments possible for anyone responsible," it read in part. "We will continue to do everything we can to stamp discrimination out of the game, but we implore government to act quickly and bring in the appropriate legislation, so this abuse has real life consequences. Social media companies need to step up and take accountability and action to ban abusers from their platforms, gather evidence that can lead to prosecution, and support making their platforms free from this type of abhorrent abuse."

Was that enough? If all of these groups follow through, maybe yes. But probably not if everyone goes back to what they were doing before without making much effort to ensure accountability. Whether real change happens in soccer remains to be seen, but campaigns like No to Racism and Kick It Out, with clear action plans by global soccer organizations, are solid starts.

For similar reasons, Lewis Hamilton set up the Hamilton Commission to investigate the lack of diversity and inclusion in motorsport. Hamilton is the most decorated person in the history of motorsport, and he accomplished that legacy in spite of the many obstacles that were placed in his way because of the sport's racism (some of which gets displayed by fans at races). Every time there is a clash of cars or a controversy that involves Hamilton, he is racially abused. There's a heavy burden on his shoulders, but he carries it with grace.

The Hamilton Commission published a report entitled "Accelerating Change: Improving Representation of Black People in UK Motorsport." Critically, while the specific goal of the commission was to look at inclusion in motorsport, its recommendations touch on education and schooling through "support and empowerment; accountability and measurement; and inspiration and engagement." Note the inclusion of the words "accountability" and "measurement." If you don't have those, you are in trouble.

All of these stories illustrate both how much progress is being made and how easy it is to backslide and lose years of hard work and struggle. But while it's essential to focus on the costs of backsliding, it's also important to note all the benefits—direct and indirect, intended and unintended—of a more equitable, inclusive society.

When one thinks about driving social change, it's natural to focus on the large costs and constraints that limit our action and possible impact. But there are also personal and systemic benefits to be gained. Although this was not my motivation, since the cabinet decision to overturn the ban on pregnant girls attending school, Sierra Leone and I personally have benefited tremendously, in multiple ways.

First, Sierra Leone gained a greater global platform when it became known for implementing an inclusive education agenda, among other important initiatives. Second, an indirect benefit of achieving and maintaining progress in one area is that it can accelerate progress in others. The ideas of radical inclusion are fast becoming second nature in Sierra Leone, spurring other progressive reforms in healthcare, gender, access to justice, and disability rights.

During debates at cabinet meetings, colleagues will regularly use the phrase "radical inclusion"—and not just the ministers of gender and children's affairs, social welfare, and youth. When the minister of energy argued that rural communities needing electricity should be given priority over urban areas for off-grid solutions, or the minister of planning and economic development called for the prioritization of women's groups in development efforts, both said "this, too, is radical inclusion."

During the COVID-19 pandemic, the government prohibited travel from one district to another. The ministry of basic and senior secondary education imposed nationwide school closures in March 2020 but, over the next six months, schools were reopened, first for students in examination classes and then finally all others. While the schools were reopening, the ministry decided that it would support the travel and relocation of students and teachers, as those trips required exceptions to the overall travel restrictions. At a late-night planning session in the ministry's conference room, we learned that only one student in a certain location had signed up for transportation support. A staff member suggested that it might not make sense to assign a vehicle to transport just this one student when there was so much demand in other areas and so few resources. As soon as those words were out of his mouth, one of our other colleagues jumped in.

"In this ministry," he said emphatically, "we believe in radical inclusion. As long as a child signed up for transportation support, she must be supported and provided for, even if she's the only one on the bus." As I sat in front of my computer, watching my staff discuss this issue together, some of them in that same conference room where these ideas of universal inclusiveness were first rejected, I no longer felt like an outsider with new ideas.

Ironically, it was the pandemic that showed us that we can always find new ways to be inclusive. I thought I'd known the scope of the problem and the various groups that had been and were still being excluded. COVID-19 taught us that our journey of learning only ends with the grave. Many of the exclusions we need to address are in plain sight right in front of us, but we don't see them. Here's just one example.

As COVID-19 devastated the world, more than one and a half billion children were forced to stay home, including my own children. Our lives were further complicated when various members of our household either tested positive for COVID-19 or needed to isolate. From my little space at home, I actively worked with my staff around the country to ensure that children were still learning, which was challenging because of large infrastructural and other inequalities.

One thing we did was expand the radio teaching program. Prior to the pandemic, the transmissions had been limited to urban areas and the content was not geared toward foundational or remedial learning. During the pandemic, we expanded the coverage to all districts via agreements with independent radio stations and provided solar-powered radio sets to students in remote areas. And we expanded the programs to cover not only core subjects, but music and meditation. For communities that did not have access to radio signals, we printed and distributed hard copies of remedial materials. For those that had access to the internet, we provided online content and special content for mobile applications. All this is why, when students in the examination classes returned to school five months later, we saw the largest number of passes in recent memory. The lesson was that we should have been doing all of this all along.

But that's the thing about transformational system change—it isn't a singular activity, a "one and done." It's like when you have a home in need of repair. First you recover your sofa. But then as you place it back in the room, you realize that the carpet has holes in it and looks shabby in comparison. So, you darn the holes in the carpet or buy a new one if you can afford it. By the time you've rehabilitated your entire home, the sofa might be in need of a repair again. Progress needs to be monitored closely, purposefully, and holistically. You are never finished, but you must be always working toward a goal.

At the start of the debates about the pregnant girls, my attention was focused on one thing only—lifting the ban that kept them out. But through the process of listening to people to understand, building large stakeholder groups, and taking action that brought about system change, we were forced to confront our own limits and those of society. We learned that there is always the danger of backlash and backsliding. But most important of all, we learned that change that promotes radical inclusion is possible.

Nearly two years after President Bio stated his unequivocal support for banning pregnant girls from schools at the Freetown International Conference Centre, the topic came up again at a lunch at the State House. We were talking about the powers and influences of development partners in shaping local policy. A lot had changed: the room decor was different, as were some of the people around the table, including a new chief minister (who was previously the minister of finance and had been an ally in the debates to overturn the ban).

For the first time, President Bio explained why he had felt compelled to make the statement in support of the ban. He had been increasingly "frustrated and annoyed" about the way the issue was being driven by external actors, he said, including some development partners who were making a change in policy a condition for receiving financing. He had chosen that moment to publicly state his opinion because representatives from all the major development partners were present, and he wanted to make the government's position clear once and for all.

The chief minister recalled that he immediately received several calls and emails from partners who assumed that the government's position had changed; many of them hadn't realized that we even had such a ban in place. I started laughing and told President Bio how strong my feelings had been as I sat in the back of that auditorium. On my first day as minister, he had thrown me the biggest challenge I could imagine. I told him that I had even considered resigning. With a smile, President Bio said, "But you like a challenge. I didn't have all the information at the time. It was not until you made its consequences clear to me across all angles that I really understood it."

You know you've won, and the ideas you fought for may just outlive you, when the people you first had to convince become even more passionate advocates than you.

There is now no greater advocate for radical inclusion than my boss, the president. When he visits villages, President Bio urges parents to keep their girls in school; in urban areas he talks to girls and their parents about menstruation and sanitary hygiene. He often references radical inclusion at cabinet discussions, urging ministers to be more expansive in their reach. At the 2021 Global Education Summit in London, where President Bio took a central role in inviting the world to raise $5 billion for education, he also promoted the message of radical inclusion, advocating for accessible, safe, and quality education for girls.

While we are on a mission to ensure that everyone can go to school and learn in a safe environment, inequalities around gender, class, income, and geography still exist. In fact, Sierra Leone's economic and development performances are among the worst in the world on some global indices, including the Human Development Index and the Human Capital Index, to name just two, largely due to low adult literacy rates and reduced quality of education. Policies that seek to help the most vulnerable—girls, the poor, those in remote regions, and citizens living with disabilities—are ways we can begin to lay the foundation for radical transformation, not just in our schools but in society as a whole. To build on that foundation, we need many more hands on deck to do the impossible. The key thing is not to slow down. We must constantly engage with our opponents, shore up our allies, and take nothing for granted as we solidify the progress we've made and continue to move forward.

We have reengaged all our stakeholders to ensure they continue to support the government's new policy position. We have provided new language and more data to religious bodies to help them support their own new positions when faced with opposition. Today, several priests speak about radical inclusion in their sermons and use the evidence that we provide. Most important for us, they also call on their congregations to take up the responsibility of protecting their girls at home and providing guidance to the boys in their communities. We certainly hope that more and more religious leaders will make this a staple of their conversations. At every opportunity, we bring in local leaders and chiefs to discuss ways in which the policy is being implemented. This shared problem-solving approach strengthens the role of stakeholders in making the policy successful and keeping it embedded in our institutions and communities.

There's one thing, though, that I try never to forget. The group that has the biggest responsibility and opportunity to instill a culture of radical inclusion are the children themselves. I saw how powerfully this can work on a trip I made to Kailahun, the district farthest from Freetown, with President Bio and the first lady. After he dedicated a new building in celebration of the seventieth anniversary of the SLPP, I joined them for lunch. The first lady, who has a background in film and communications and plays a major role in her husband's political campaigns, was scheduled to distribute sanitary hygiene kits at a school immediately after lunch. She asked me if I'd like to come along, and a few minutes later we were on our way.

The sequence of these programs is usually some speeches,

a musical or comedic interlude, a keynote by the first lady, and finally, the distribution of the items she's brought. That day I gave an impromptu speech, then a national musical star, Markmuday, took the microphone to entertain the students. The energy of the place was ignited. All the students had their hands up, dancing and miming to the lyrics of his songs.

That was when I saw two girls approach the stage, one holding the hand of the other. Next thing I knew, they were dancing with Markmuday. One had a cane and the other didn't. Just before the student without the cane went back down into the audience, she fixed the button on her friend's uniform. That's when I realized the girl with the cane was blind. Her friend had helped her on stage so she could be in the center of the event and dance with a pop star. Soon, another girl with a physical disability was also on the stage. At this point, the first lady and I were wiping tears from our eyes. All she could say was, "Wow." To watch these girls dance with Markmuday, at an event on girls' education and welfare in one of the poorest and remotest districts in Sierra Leone, is what the policy of radical inclusion in schools is all about.

It's what radical inclusion is about no matter where it happens.

Afterword

·····

I am still learning.

—ATTRIBUTED TO MICHELANGELO
(AT AGE EIGHTY-SEVEN)

If my transition to public service was unexpected and surprising for many, what was especially shocking to us all, including me, was the speed with which I rose to the top as a senior cabinet minister in charge of the government's flagship portfolios of education and innovation. I, too, had previously believed that I was too young, too technical, and too different from other government officials to thrive in political rooms.

Today, I've learned tremendously about the ins and outs of public service and how to get difficult things done. But it's

229

not been easy. I've tried to share with you what I've learned in a land that might be very far from yours, in the hopes that some of my experiences may help you in your own efforts to drive change, wherever you live and no matter what kinds of exclusions you are hoping to remedy.

As a final word, I want to share three important things I've learned about people—those who are excluded and their excluders; those who are part of the status quo and those on the margin; those who are changemakers and those who are silent observers.

First, people like changemakers and mavericks, but only from afar. How we dress, how we talk, what we say, how we walk, and other external factors that have nothing to do with our core beings are all markers that others use to decide whose voices to listen to. People decide whether they will support the causes you advocate and fight for according to whether they feel you are one of them. As someone who has been systematically categorized as an outsider both abroad and at home, I have come to realize that the strongest defenders of the status quo are the people who benefit from it the most.

The way we fight for justice and inclusion is not by assimilating and being like everyone else, but by being different, understanding our differences, and recognizing how they may be used against us. Change-making is not easy. Those who dedicate their lives to it are fated to be classed as "weird" before they are accepted, if they ever are. You are weird because you are going against the grain and are fighting against something others either don't see or believe is right. What really helps is your own comfort in being different.

Second, people believe in change, but often only as an idea that does not affect them and the status quo. This is because bringing about change can be demanding and exact great costs.

In general discussions about inclusion, it is often incorrectly assumed that it is only those who are doing the excluding that don't want change. But the status quo—for the excluder and those being excluded—is hard to change because most people like routines and do not enjoy learning and doing new things, particularly when they are linked to changes in culture, tradition, or religion. Changing the status quo requires new ways of thinking and doing that have associated financial and social costs that even people with the best intentions may decide are more than they can afford. It is thus very important to reach out to the silent observers, those who sit in the middle and don't think of themselves as perpetrators. These are, for example, the colleagues at work who may not actively exclude interns from activities but would not invite them to sit in on a meeting where they might make contacts and learn.

For people to imagine that change is possible, they need role models. While the data, evidence, and logic may align in favor of inclusion, the best way to effect it is through action and modeling. To continue to solidify the principles of radical inclusion, we need more religious and civic leaders and ordinary people at work and home to champion it and promote its practices.

Third, people who are aware of unjust systems often don't believe that it's their role to change them. When we started the fight to allow pregnant girls in school, it wasn't just us who knew this was a fight for justice that went beyond a single type of exclusion. Our opponents, too, were thinking beyond pregnant girls—would he soon start advocating for gay rights in schools? It was a fight that we would lose before we started unless we were *radical* in just about everything we did: the use of data and evidence, our social engagements and citizen consultations, speaking up to authority, swimming against the tide, and more. But we still needed the civil servants and the cabinet to understand and support our ideas. We needed specifically to transform our mentors into allies, and the silent observers who believed that things needed to change into activists.

The biggest transformations happened when directors and ordinary staff began pressing for radical inclusion. Once President Bio—the person who ultimately had the most leverage to drive change from within the system—was engaged, the change came about much quicker than anticipated. That is not to say that all the previous years of community advocacy were not important, but it was led from outside the system. You need people within the system, those sitting on the inclusion-exclusion barrier, to be active players, too.

There are still incredibly difficult challenges of inclusion and equity in education and in society around the world. Disability, mental health, poverty, religion, and gender still limit access to education and full participation in social and civic life for significant parts of our population.

But I'm hopeful for the future.

Recently, I went back to Bo to visit my mom. I was taking a walk around the compound, drinking a cup of fresh lemongrass tea, when I saw a young woman on her way to the well. She had two children with her, one walking behind her and another on her back. The boy walking had a ball in his hand. When they returned from the well, the bucket of water was perfectly balanced on her head. One hand gently touched the bucket, and the other was held by the boy with the ball. It was Aminata, the girl who had shared her hopes with me at the start of this journey. I said hello to her and asked about her baby. The baby was doing well; it was named after her grandmother. I was conscious that she had a heavy weight on her head, so I quickly asked the question I most wanted to: Had she dropped out of school and if so, would she re-enroll?

She smiled and said, "Thank you for asking, sir. I went to my village to have my child—but then I came back here and enrolled in school. I'll be taking the senior school certification exams this year so I can continue my education."

As her education continues, so does mine. And I hope yours does, too. That's the final thing I want to add about radical inclusion. Only when you are a lifelong student of it can you possibly be doing it right.

Acknowledgments

. . . . .

This book would not be possible without many people's efforts and contributions. There are too many to list here and I am truly grateful for all of you—thank you.

But there are a few specific people who deserve special mentions, so please permit me to mention them.

First, thank you to my family—my wife, Kate Krontiris, and children Nyaanina Krontiris-Sengeh and Peynina Krontiris-Sengeh, my niece Kadija Davida Conteh, my parents Paul Sengeh and Elizabeth Sengeh, my siblings, and all my extended family. You are my greatest source of love, support, and hope—no one believes in me more than you. Thank you for continuing to allow me to break rules and rewrite them.

Second, President Bio deserves a special commendation. He not only challenged me to think about service to Sierra Leone at a time when no one believed I was ready for it, he then served me the hardest professional challenge ever when he confirmed the ban on pregnant girls from attending school on my first day as a cabinet minister. He has been an incredible leader, teacher, mentor, and friend to me over the years and I remain committed to our shared vision to transform Sierra Leone.

Third, I would like to thank my friends from my professional, graduate, undergraduate, and high school life who have continued to shape my thinking (including reading various drafts of this book and the thousand bad ideas I bombard you with). I have used many lessons from our shared experiences. My life is richer because of you and this book was written with you in mind.

Fourth, my agent, Kathy Robbins, and editor, Will Schwalbe, have been phenomenal in helping me share this story. Thank you to the publishing team at Flatiron, especially Bob Miller, Samantha Zukergood, Megan Lynch, and Amelia Possanza. Special shout-out to Arthur Goldwag and Alexandra Sugarman for your editorial support. Thank you for the journey. All errors are mine and the really nice insights are influenced by their questions and suggestions.

Finally, this book wouldn't be here without the people of Sierra Leone and especially my staff at the ministry of basic and senior secondary education and the directorate of science, technology, and innovation. Grace Kargobai deserves special mention because of her incredible passion, dedication, and kindness. I am able to do all I can do in my work because of the support I get from Grace.

I want to end by thanking all the children of Sierra Leone—those whom I serve. I am so excited about the future because I know that Sierra Leone will continue to transform its education sector in fundamental ways that place every learner at the heart of its reforms.

Credits

·····

Grateful acknowledgment is made to the following for permission to reprint the previously published material included in chapter epigraphs:

Chapter 1 (page 17): *Just Mercy* by Bryan Stevenson (© 2014 by Bryan Stevenson, published by Spiegel & Grau).

Chapter 2 (page 47): *Daring Greatly* by Brené Brown (© 2012 by Brené Brown, published by Avery).

Chapter 3 (page 77): *The Path Made Clear* by Oprah Winfrey (© 2019 by Oprah Winfrey, published by Flatiron Books).

Chapter 4 (page 103): *Nelson Mandela by Himself* by Nelson Mandela (© 2011 by Nelson Mandela, published by MacMillan South Africa).

Chapter 5 (page 137): "Lose Yourself" by Eminem (© 2014 Aftermath Records).

Chapter 6 (page 167): *All About Love* by bell hooks (© 1999 by bell hooks, published by William Morrow).

About the Author

David Moinina Sengeh is the minister of basic and senior secondary education and chief innovation officer for the government of Sierra Leone. He holds a bachelor's degree and a PhD in biomedical engineering from Harvard College and MIT respectively. He is a TED Fellow, a World Economic Forum Young Global Leader, an Obama Foundation Leaders Africa Fellow, and was included on the 2013 *Forbes* 30 Under 30 list. Sengeh serves as chair of the Global Education Monitoring Report to UNESCO. *Radical Inclusion* is his first book.

**MOMENT
OF LIFT**
BOOKS

Moment of Lift Books, created by Melinda French Gates
in partnership with Flatiron Books,
is an imprint dedicated to publishing original nonfiction
by visionaries working to unlock a more equal world
for women and girls.

To learn more about Moment of Lift Books,
visit momentoflift.com.